Hero on a stolen horse

Hero on a stolen horse

The highwayman and his brothers-in-arms the bandit and the bushranger

HILARY AND MARY EVANS

With illustrations from the Mary Evans Picture Library

FREDERICK MULLER LIMITED LONDON

First published in Great Britain 1977
by Frederick Muller Limited, London,
NW2 6LE

ISBN 0 584 10340 9

British Library Cataloguing in Publication Data

Evans, Hilary
    Hero on a stolen horse.
    1. Brigands and robbers—History
    I. Title II. Evans, Mary, b.1936
    364.1′55′09   HV6441

    ISBN 0-584-10340-9

Phototypeset by Computer Photoset Ltd., Birmingham
Printed and bound by: Robert MacLehose & Co. Ltd., Glasgow

Contents

Preface

Even while he waited for execution morning, the condemned highwayman of 18th century England was visited in his cell by the fashionable ladies of London. Even while he robbed and murdered, the Australian bushranger's praises were being sung in admiring ballads which told of his courage and generosity. When the American train-robber had finally been gunned down for a dead-or-alive reward, men were proud to claim acquaintance with one who, they insisted, had never taken from the poor, but gave them what he took from the rich. Balkan banditti, two hundred years dead, are today a treasured part of national folklore. Robin Hood, Butch Cassidy and the Sundance Kid, Ned Kelly, Salvatore Giuliano, have been not just the subjects of recent films but their heroes — presented to us as brave and noble, worthy of our sympathy and admiration. Why?

Not every kind of criminal has received this sort of treatment. Few of us, even if we know any pickpockets or rapists, are inclined to boast of the acquaintance. Are there any popular songs in praise of counterfeiters or embezzlers? Yet in many different parts of the world, at many different periods of history, certain criminals have been singled out for hero status: in almost every case they have been men who made their living as highway robbers, preying on the traveller whether on foot or on horseback, journeying by stagecoach or railway train. Why?

Many of these men also indulged in other forms of criminal activity; sometimes highway robbery was only a minor part of their careers. But it was as highway robbers that they were known and admired. A century and a half ago the historian Macaulay said of the English Highwayman that 'he held an aristocratical position in the community of thieves'. So it was with his brothers-in-arms in almost every part of the world. Why?

This book sets out to find the answers to these questions. To attempt to do so by making a comprehensive study of every recorded highway robber would not only be tedious but, by its weight of detail—fact or fiction—would confuse the issue. Each of the groups we shall be looking at—whether English Highwaymen or American train-robbers, Australian bushrangers or Italian brigands—have already had whole books devoted to them, and so have many of the individuals within the groups. The ghosts of Robin Hood and Ned Kelly must be amazed at the substantial bibliographies they can boast today: the stories of Dick Turpin and Jesse James have been told sufficiently often to satisfy the vanities even of such vain men. So we have had to select. On the one hand we have picked out some of the best known individuals in each category simply *because* they are the best known: we wonder what it was about these particular individuals that made the public select them, and not others, for special admiration? And on the other hand, we have chosen others less well known, some for comparison with the archetypes, some because they offer features of particular interest which throw light on their profession as a whole.

The information gathered here has been drawn from many old accounts, and these accounts seldom agree with one another. Events are in different orders, dates vary—was Cottington killed in 1656 or 1659, was Parsons arrested at Hounslow or Brentford? Probably no amount of research now could establish these facts, for there are no certain primary sources to consult. So we have done our best to establish coherent accounts, discarding stories that are clearly incompatible with the rest: when we have had to make a choice between one version and an equally well attested alternative, we have tried to choose the one most consistent with what we know of its hero.

But in any case, ultimately the legend is more important than the original facts. Where Dick Turpin was born is less significant than the question why this sordid little petty criminal came to be credited with other men's feats and so raised to a place in history far above his deserts. But then so, in greater or lesser degree, it was with all the characters who appear in this book. Each presents a different facet of the same enigma.

Stealing the profits of other men's labour to fill his belly and pay for his drink and his whores—stealing even the guns he needs to steal with and the horse that carries him safely away from the scenes of his crimes—raping and looting and murdering his way to the scaffold, the highwayman isn't, on the face of it, much of an ornament to society. So how has he managed to charm his way into so many of society's good books, what strange power does he possess to throw dust in society's disapproving eyes? Why are we all so fascinated by this hero on the stolen horse?

Acknowledgements

A very substantial literature has been devoted to the Highwayman and his colleagues. Most of it is repetitive, little goes beneath the surface to explore the motives behind the myth. I would like therefore particularly to mention E. J. Hobsbawm's brief but thoughtful BANDITS (Weidenfeld & Nicolson 1969). Others of more than average interest are:–

John Bellamy, CRIME AND PUBLIC ORDER IN ENGLAND IN THE LATER MIDDLE AGES (Routledge 1973)

Thomas S. Duke, CELEBRATED CRIMINAL CASES OF AMERICA (James H. Barry Co. 1910)

Robert Elman, BADMEN OF THE WEST (Ridge Press 1974)

Charles Harper, HALF HOURS WITH THE HIGHWAYMEN (Chapman & Hall 1908)

William Joy & Tom Palmer, THE BUSHRANGERS (Shakespeare Head Press, Sydney, 1963)

David Rowan, FAMOUS EUROPEAN CASES (Frederick Muller 1956)

Patrick Pringle, STAND AND DELIVER (Museum Press 1951)

I would also like to record my gratitude to the London Library, but for whose facilities my task would have been infinitely more laborious.

Note

There is no one label to cover all the species of criminal with which this book is concerned. For the sake of convenience, therefore, the word 'highwayman' is used throughout as the basic term, but it must be understood that, unless otherwise indicated, it refers to highway predators of all kinds, not simply to those who operated in 17th and 18th century England. Where reference is specifically intended to these latter and no other, the word is used with a capital 'H'.

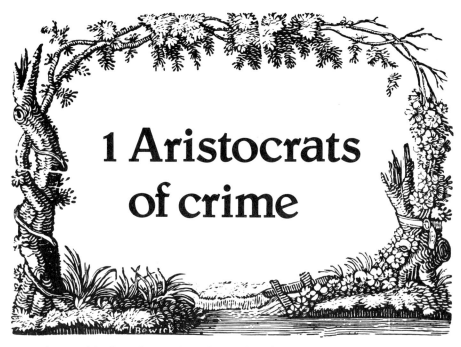

1 Aristocrats of crime

They robbed and raped and murdered. They lied and cheated, betrayed and deceived. When it served their purpose, they stole a man's property, used his wife or his daughter, destroyed his home and livelihood, took his life. When they gave, it was only a bribe; when they showed consideration, it was to buy goodwill. If they claimed to have been unjustly treated by society, it was to justify themselves for flouting society's rules; when they claimed to be revenging themselves on society for its injustice, they took their revenge on the weak and innocent more often than on those who had allegedly caused the injustice.

Yet to many they were, and still are, heroes. They became legends in their own lifetimes, and to later generations they have become part of folk history. There is probably no nation which does not number, among its pantheon of popular heroes, some outlaw who defied the establishment of his day, who robbed and murdered his way to enduring fame. Sardinia has its bandits and England its Highwaymen, Australia its Bushrangers and India its Thugs, Italy its brigands and America its train-robbers. Juro Janosik of Slovakia, Jesse James of the American West, Scotty Smith of the Transvaal, Robin Hood of Sherwood Forest, Tiburcio Vasquez from Mexico, Ned Kelly of Ireland and Australia, Dick Turpin of England, Salvatore Giuliano of Sicily—each has his permanent place now in the legends of his countrymen, the subject not only of popular ballads and catchpenny biographies, but of scholarly treatises and serious movies.

1

Claude Duval as 'Penny
Dreadful' hero.

THE PARAGON LIBRARY.

 DEEDS OF DARING AND CHIVALRY.

COMPLETE ONE PENNY.

CLAUDE DU VAL
THE DASHING KNIGHT OF THE ROAD.

LONDON: A. RITCHIE and Co., Red Lion Court, Fleet Street.

Yet each of these highwaymen, when you strip off the fancy dress, is revealed as a parasite on society who robbed, raped, murdered, lied, cheated, betrayed, deceived. Not one of them ever lifted a finger to help a fellow man except to further his own interests; apart from enriching the world's stock of folklore, not one left the world a better or happier place. And yet, for all his shortcomings, the highwayman was better suited than anyone else to provide a model for the folk hero that society needs.

Why the highwayman? Man has shown himself extraordinarily inventive in devising types of crime, but only a very few have earned the sympathy of their fellow men. Interest, yes: there is a perennial fascination with most kinds of crime, so that books about murderers and forgers, thieves and confidence men are always sure of a sale. But Crippen and Jack the Ripper, Landru and Kruger,

Claude Duval salutes his
victims: The Highwayman
as hero. (Wood engraving
from drawing by Howard
Pyle)

2

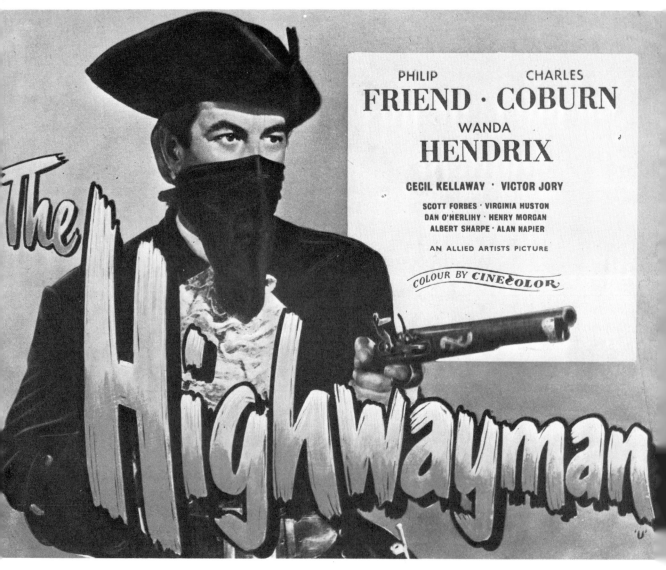

PHILIP
CHARLES
FRIEND · COBURN

WANDA
HENDRIX

CECIL KELLAWAY · VICTOR JORY

SCOTT FORBES · VIRGINIA HUSTON
DAN O'HERLIHY · HENRY MORGAN
ALBERT SHARPE · ALAN NAPIER

AN ALLIED ARTISTS PICTURE

COLOUR BY **CINECOLOR**

The Highwayman

The myth survives. Philip Friend cocks his pistol in *The Highwayman* based on Alfred Noyes' poem of the same title.

though the subjects of biographies and films, were never popular heroes. And it is significant that in these cases it is always on the individual that interest is focussed—not on poisoners as a whole, but on Madeleine Smith in particular; not swindlers in general, but Ivan Kruger especially.

There have, it's true, been certain categories of criminal who have achieved a reputation as a class: there are the original Assassins of medieval Asia, the garotters of Victorian London, the rum-runners of prohibition America. But notoriety isn't the same as hero-worship. The Buccaneers of the Spanish Main came closest, but nobody has seriously sought to make heroic figures out of a gang of ruffians so obviously evil. So it has come about that only highwaymen, as a class, have found widespread sympathy and admiration.

Often a hero becomes a projection of what some part of us, consciously or unconsciously, would like to be. As we shall see, the highwayman carries out this role supremely well, representing many of our hopes and aspirations, and at the same time symbolising escape from many of our oppressions and frustrations. But, for all his alleged virtues, the highwayman is fundamentally anti-social and while part of us admires, another part shakes its head in disapproval. When looking for heroes, we choose sinners more often than saints. After all, if we chose a saint, what excuse would we have for not following in his steps, giving up all sorts of comforts and enjoyments? With a flawed hero such as the highwayman, we can admire, then turn back—albeit with a sigh—to the familiar, comfortable patterns of our own lives.

Nevertheless, the highwayman does not come to us ready-made for the part we want him to play. The facts need a little tailoring here and there. Throughout this book we shall continually be seeing how the real-life highwayman has been transformed into the legendary hero. So let us start by looking at the highwayman as a species, in all his varieties, and see what are the qualities which have made him so suitable as raw material for heroic legend.

The highwayman thrives in a time-and-place situation which is one of comparative lawlessness. Not complete lawlessness; for then there'd be no law-abiding victims for him to prey on; he'd merely be competing with other outlaws like himself. His very livelihood depends on there being enough law and order to keep a steady supply of loot passing within his reach—an ecological system like that which determines whether a particular natural environment can sustain lions or eagles, and in what numbers.

So the highwayman flourishes best in places and periods where a framework of law and order exists, but one which is either still rudimentary, or is not too rigorously imposed. In 14th century England, for instance, the machinery of law had to a large extent collapsed because of rivalry between the court and the local lords: in this situation it was possible for bands of brigands, such as that of Robin Hood, to operate with considerable freedom. Slovakia in the 1700s, Greece in the 1890s, Sicily in the 1950s, all presented eco-systems similarly favourable to the right kind of opportunist.

Of all environments the most favourable is the developing country, where the march of civilisation has created a structure of law and order, but where the machinery isn't yet operating effectively. We shall find our highwaymen exploiting this kind of situation in 19th century Australia, in South Africa at the time of the Transvaal Gold Rush, in the Western states of America throughout the period of intensive settlement.

But we shall see the situation at its most delicately balanced in 17th and 18th century England. Here, compared with Australia and America, a well-developed structure of law and order existed, but there was just sufficient room for manoeuvre to enable the Highwayman to function. Not in the massive gangs of medieval England or Janosik's Slovakia; nor for the years of free-range plundering of Jesse James' Missouri or Ned Kelly's Australia: but within narrow limits which imposed tight conditions on the English Highwayman and made him the most finely contrived of all robber heroes.

The environment in which the highwayman operated had generally one other very important characteristic. The central authority was likely to be one which could be seen, not simply as the outlaw's natural enemy, but also as being in some degree hostile or, at any rate, unsympathetic to the entire community among whom the highwayman lived. This created a 'them-us' dichotomy which he was able to exploit to his advantage. We shall see this operating in various ways in different countries and at different periods. The peasants of 14th century England were oppressed by local barons who came between them and central justice. The populations of 19th century Greece and Bulgaria were subjected to a totally hostile Turkish dominion against which local bandits could paint themselves as heroic patriots. The country people of Sicily and Sardinia, even to this day, feel little or no allegiance to a remote and unsympathetic central government. Social attitudes in 19th century Australia were conditioned by the warder-prisoner relationship, a hangover from those early convict days. Settlers in the American West resented the big financial interests—the railroad magnates with their powerful lobbies in Washington—who they saw as ruthless landgrabbers sanctioned by a corrupt federal government. Even in 18th century England the Highwayman was able to take advantage of a social climate which reflected, though in a far subtler way, the same conflict between local and wider allegiances, a contest between the rights of individual man and the claims of the leviathan state.

In order to make the most of this situation, it stood the highwayman in good stead if he was himself of humble origin. Few of the heroes we shall meet in this book were of aristocratic or even gentle birth: the great majority rose from the lowest ranks, where existence itself was a matter of perpetual struggle, and where life tended to be lived permanently on the edge of the law. In such an environment those who have to enforce the law come to be seen as a

The bandit hero—Italy's Rosolino Pilo personifies the romantic ideal. (Barbieri portrait)

natural enemy: from covert to open war is only a short step.

Many circumstances can supply the impulse to take that short step. It can be a grievance, genuine or fancied, such as sent the Sontag Brothers into their private vendetta against the American railroads. It can be the grinding hopelessness that faces many returned soldiers after a war, particularly if they happen to have been on the losing side, such as many Cavalier soldiers after the death of Charles I or American adventurers in the South after the Civil War. Or it can simply be the prospect of a better life—more money, higher status—such as inspired Captain Maclean or Sixteen-String Jack Rann in 18th century England.

All this could have been said with equal truth of the urban criminal—the burglar, the pickpocket and the street racketeer. But such men did not become heroes except, very rarely, on a strictly local basis. This was where his country cousin started to have the advantage over him; for the entire scenario of circumstances in which the highwayman pursued his career contributed to make him a sympathetic, heroic character, compared with the city criminal.

To start with, the highwayman was generally forced to adopt a nomadic way of life, living from hand to mouth, always on the move to evade pursuit, hiding out with his gang for a while in some remote sanctuary, then moving on, on, and on again, looking for some resting place where the law wouldn't be breathing so hard down his neck. A few, like Sicily's Salvatore Giuliano or Ireland's Jeremiah Grant, managed to win enough local sympathy to be able to live in their native district for some years on end; but even they had to live, not in farms or even cottages, but in secret hiding-places which could hardly have been more comfortable than Dick Turpin's cave in Epping Forest or Robin Hood's in Sherwood.

Such discomfort, of course, helped to generate popular sympathy. Because he had no wealth to flaunt, it was possible to believe that the highwayman had given all his takings to the poor and needy—or at least, that he had taken only sufficient for his needs, and bestowed the balance in worthy causes. No cliché is commoner in the stories of highwaymen than that they stole from the rich to give to the poor. As we shall see, this was hardly ever true: and when it did seem to be true, the generosity was likely to be a calculated one. In practice, the highwayman was almost certain to spend the fruits of his crimes on himself, in wild orgies of wine and women; then, when it was all spent, to take to the road again. Yet even when this was known to be the case, it could be seen as 'human' and therefore excusable. To spend money on drink and gambling and whores is always more attractive than salting it away in a bank. Especially if you make a living by robbing banks.

Those highwaymen who have been able to identify themselves in the public mind with some sympathetic political cause have, of course, a ready-made excuse for stealing. The political kidnappers of our own day are widely admired because the ransoms they demand are supposedly intended to further their political aims. Perhaps they are sincere: I am in no position to say for sure that today's political terrorists are using their political motivations as a front for old-fashioned robbery. But hard and fast lines aren't easy to draw: Juro Janosik became a symbol of Slovakian patriotism, Salvatore Giuliano saw himself as the saviour of his native Sicily. Did they believe in their own claims? Nobody now can say for sure. But like Australia's Ned Kelly and Mexico's Joaquin Murieta, they were undoubtedly able to take advantage of the ambiguity. If the highwayman can blur the line between robber and patriot, he can hope to enjoy popular support—at best positive assistance, at the least a reluctance to assist his pursuers. Such support can make a world of difference to the effectiveness of his operations and the length of his career.

Once the highwayman has been established in a favourable light, excuses are found for his taking to a criminal career in the first place. With a philanthropic or patriotic or political cloak thrown over his acts of robbery, murder and so forth, it becomes easy enough to admire other aspects of his way of life. The very fact that he dwells in the open helps him to represent our private dreams:

In Summer, when the shaws be shine,
　and leaves be large and long,
it is full merry in fair Forest
　to hear the fowles song.
To see the Deer draw to the dale,
　and leave the hilles hee,
and shadow them in the leaves green
　under the greenwood tree.
Robin Hood and the Monk

We all know—or most of us do, at any rate—that we are better off, all things considered, as parts of the social machine, playing our roles in society, contributing to its running and being paid in return. We subscribe to the code that it is better to earn our own bread than to steal other people's. But this social contract is achieved only with a certain amount of sacrifice—of independence given up, of personal initiative resigned. In order to obtain the rewards and privileges of belonging to an ordered community, with its streetlamps and refuse collections and public libraries and police patrols, we have to give up a great deal that is deep and powerful in our natures. And—at least subconsciously—we cannot but resent this; and our resentment is turned not on ourselves, but on the social establishment which seems to have forced us into making our sacrifice. At the same time we continue to feel more than a twinge of envy for those who dare to opt out of the system, who refuse to sign the slightly shameful deal that we have signed. Not that we would, if the crunch came, wish to be one of them. Nice though it would be to pay no rates, to live with women as long as we chose then move on to the next, to wake in the morning with no office or factory to clock into, few of us think it worth while giving up our jobs as chartered accountants or dentists or schoolteachers in return for such freedom. And yet the lure remains, perpetually tantalising . . .

This is the impulse behind Jean Jacques Rousseau's concept of the Noble Savage, that wonderful creation of the 18th century intellectual; or the Byronic Hero, the fantasy product of the succeeding Romantic Movement. Like them, the highwayman and the bandit, if not born free, have found freedom: like them, they stand for a world lost to us civilised men and women, a natural world, a world somehow more 'real' than the concrete and plastic artifact we have chosen.

But of course it's not quite so simple. Just to be natural and primitive isn't enough: despite Rousseau, you can't make heroes out of Australian aborigines or Amazon headhunters. Certain conditions must be met. Compare the Highwayman of 18th century England with his predecessors and his successors. The medieval footpad, lurking in the shadow of the hedgerow to leap on the passing wayfarer as he trudges along the muddy track with his donkey—somehow he's hardly the stuff that heroes are made of. The stocking-masked gang of our own age, ambushing a security van on a motorway spur with teargas grenades; they have their own picturesque qualities, no doubt, but they just don't have the charisma of the mounted horseman whose place of work was not the M5 or the A31, but the King's Highway, waiting silently in the moonlight under pine trees sighing in the night wind, cocked hat pulled low over masked face, pistol in either hand, leaning forward the better to hear the first rumble of the approaching stagecoach.

Perhaps more than anything else, it was the horse that supplied the essential ingredient of magic. We all share an atavistic feeling that the man who loves horses cannot be wholly evil. The difference that distinguishes the dashing hussar from the plodding infantryman, the cowboy from the ploughboy, Sir Lancelot du Lac from the common adulterer—this difference distinguishes the highwayman from the footpad or the motorway bandit. The true hero of Dick Turpin's Ride to York is Black Bess.

And so it's on his horse that the highwayman comes riding into town on Saturday night, to drink a few bottles with the friendly or frightened neighbours and visit his girl and buy his supplies; and then he rides back into the hills, back to his life of crime. And somehow even his crimes don't seem so reprehensible as the crimes of the city criminal. To be mugged in a back-alley off Main Street is simply squalid. To be held up on the Abilene Trail, on a bright morning in God's great out-of-doors, is something else. Property is property, true; yet circumstances do seem to alter cases. Somehow there is an innocence about relieving a man of his possessions in the open country. As though he had, by venturing abroad in the first place, accepted a challenge: in losing his property he's simply lost his gamble, that's all. And if what's lost is gold or silver dug up out of the ground—ground that belongs to all men alike, notwithstanding some trivial legalistic claims—why, stealing gold and silver is hardly stealing at all!

Nonetheless, men are apt to resist those who try to steal it; and in the process men get shot on both sides. As far as possible, the hero legends make out that the highwayman killed only in self-defence—for few, very very few, never killed at all (California's Black Bart was one—he even carried an unloaded gun!). Generally the legends have a hard time with their heroes' killings, however generously they give the highwayman the benefit of the 'self-defence' doubt. Even if you are ready to accept that every one of Salvatore Giuliano's hundred or more police victims was killed in self defence, was the same true of his eighty three civilian victims?

But killing is between man and man, and can be seen as a part of the job, a 'natural' process, like the way lions have to kill zebras. So the legends tend to skate easily over the murders. On a more personal level, the hero is invested with a selection of the regular virtues—he is loyal, trustworthy, dependable, a man of his word. He is nearly always courteous to women—Ned Kelly, that devoted son, provides a particularly striking example of a trait that is claimed for most highwaymen. The older highwaymen were generally pious—we shall see what risks Robin Hood took in order to hear Mass regularly. When the government deserves loyalty, the highwayman is loyal—Robin Hood, though he opposed the local law officers, willingly bowed the knee before his rightful King, and the English Highwaymen of the 17th century were generally depicted as men whose worst fault had been to be too loyal to their rightful King Charles I.

Waiting for the scaffold. Gill Smith in chains. (*Newgate Calendar*)

Gibbets were set up in the Highwaymen's favourite haunts as a deterrent: these bodies mouldering in their chains were displayed on Hounslow Heath. (Engraved from a drawing by Dodd for *The Newgate Calendar*)

But, inevitably, sooner or later the highwayman was caught. The English Highwayman seldom survived more than a year or two, often much less. The American train robbers, with wider country to escape into, stayed clear of the law for longer, but it caught up with them all in the end. The great Slovakian hero Janosik had only two years in which to build the reputation which has already lasted two centuries. And the end of their careers was, of course, an essential part of the legend. It is almost as though this was a condition of their being elevated to hero status: as though society made a bargain with them. Look, we will make a hero of you, forget your evil deeds and praise your virtues, write ballads in your honour and make films about you, but in return, you must allow us to hang you.

It is noteworthy that it was during their final weeks on earth that the English Highwaymen tasted the sweetest fruits of their career—that is, when they were safely under lock and key, and already condemned to death. In those last few weeks between their sentence and its execution, they lived as heroes, feted and visited, honoured and lauded:

Methinks I see him already in the Cart, sweeter and more lovely than the Nosegay in his Hand!—I hear the Crowd extolling his Resolution and Intrepidity!—What Vollies of Sighs are sent from the Windows of Holborn, that so comely a Youth should be brought to disgrace!—I see him at the Tree! The whole Circle are in Tears!—even Butchers weep!—Jack Ketch himself hesitates to perform his duty, and would be glad to lose his Fee by a Reprieve!

(*Polly, in Gay's The Beggar's Opera*)

But in fact nobody wanted the highwayman to be reprieved: his death is a vital part of his legend, the climax that gives it its value, like the end of Antigone or Othello or Aida. Robin Hood must die betrayed by the Abbess of Kirklees: Salvatore Giuliano must die, betrayed by one of his own lieutenants. We would not wish them to have survived. Jesse James, gunned down by a faithless confederate for a few dollars reward, died a better death than his brother Frank who died two score years later, a farmer, in his own bed. Ned Kelly, shooting his way through the ranks of police in his desperate last bid, when he might have made his own getaway by deserting his comrades, made the bravest end of all. Yet, despite those many pleas for mercy as he lay in the condemned cell, we would not wish him to have been pardoned for his robberies and murders. Though we have that deep yearning for the outlaw's free-ranging life, we are glad to have a reason for believing we did better to opt for the safety of life within the law. And there, dancing on the end of a rope at the age of thirty, is our reason.

2 'Robyn Hode and his meynie'

It was a world where all respectable folk lived behind walls—in walled towns, walled castles, walled farms. Between one walled community and the next, slow tracks wandered through wild forests and over savage heaths, tracks of grass and mud, not designed for speed even if any vehicles capable of speed had existed.

This was the face of the land in medieval England; comparable conditions, with regional variations, existed all over medieval Europe. Such conditions favoured any man who chose to take to highway robbery, and in medieval Europe highway robbery was the safest if not the most rewarding of criminal careers.

Medieval society, in principle so neatly ordered into Church, Court and Commons, was in fact anything but stable. Wars, international and civil, crusades, plagues, all disturbed the equilibrium of social life. Weak central governments gave power-hungry nobles the opportunity either to set up local despotisms of their own or to combine in power-bids against the government itself. A man was hard put to know where to bestow his allegiance—on the divinely sanctioned but distant king, the local secular authorities who might or might not be serving the king's will, or the ecclesiastical powers who were often the most effective because they were the most durable element in society. By supporting one, it was easy to fall foul of the others. On a large scale, this could lead to one of the periodic social uprisings of the medieval age—the Peasants' Revolt in 14th century England, or the similar Jacquerie in France.

On the individual level, it could send a man flying into the relative safety of the open country, out of reach of the authorities, there to make his way as best he could, an outlaw, with every man's hand against him.

The chances of actually being caught by the law were small: there was little law enforcement outside the towns. Just how little is shown in this comment by the medieval historian John Bellamy, who tells us that 'not one investigator has been able to indicate even a few years of effective policing in the period 1290–1485'. During this period, references to outlaw gangs turn up frequently in the records, though with a frustrating lack of detail. We can only surmise that they were often discharged soldiers, banding together and using their military skills to get them a living which they could not easily find in the towns where the trade guilds had a stranglehold on the most profitable occupations. Sometimes they were downright criminals on the run from justice. Sometimes they were simple opportunists, working on their own behalf or underwritten by outwardly respectable authorities, barons or bishops, much as the

Robbers attacking a traveller, by Hans Ulrich Franck, 1543. The scene is set in Germany, but it could have been matched anywhere throughout Europe at this period.

Mafia operates in more modern times. (There is at least one instance of a religious house actually taking to robbery itself: in December 1317 six monks from Rufford Abbey, in Nottinghamshire, were charged with robbing a traveller and holding him for ransom!).

Highway robbery appealed to the outlaw not only because it was one of the few ways of life which could be practised without braving the dangers of the towns, so small, compact and densely populated as to be virtually self-policing. Highway robbery was also relatively easy. Within the walled communities a man was at least partially secure; but as soon as he left the town gates and ventured onto those ill-kept tracks, he put himself severely at risk.

Those who built the tracks did what they could. They kept to the crests of hills as much as possible, avoiding the more heavily wooded valleys and so diminishing the risk of ambush. Where local authorities had sufficient power, they could order the vegetation on either side of the way to be cleared, again to cut down potential hiding places and give the traveller greater warning of impending attack.

Acts of Parliament encouraged local authorities into action. The Statute of Winchester of 1285, confirmed and extended in 1354, made local authorities responsible for compensating travellers for losses incurred within their areas, unless the robbers were caught within forty days. This applied only during daylight hours, and not on Sundays when no respectable person would be travelling anyway. In the 16th century the Statute was amended to make the local authorities responsible for only half the sum lost, so great an imposition was it on the ratepayer. Even so, in 1590 the Hundred of Benhurst paid out £255 compensation for robberies in Maidenhead Thicket alone; no small sum in those days.

But the traveller was expected to do what he could to protect himself. Whenever possible he would find companions on his journey, as did Chaucer's Canterbury Pilgrims; he would wait at inns for suitable companions, and they would set out together. Naturally they went armed, and the servants that accompanied them were armed also. They travelled only by day and made sure of getting to the next town before the gates were closed at nightfall: in those days the phrase 'a day's journey' was a tautology, for every 'journey' was what the word implies, a day's travel.

The great majority of people, of course, didn't travel at all. Most medieval people had no notion of what the world was really like beyond the horizon, let alone over the mountain ranges or across the sea. Those who went voyaging could bring back whatever wonderful tales they chose; truth or fiction alike would be met with wonder and incredulity.

But others had no option but to travel. Infirm though the central government might be, it still had to function. The king had to get his revenues, and so his tax collectors had to bring them to him. Merchants had to travel with their goods; courtiers had to take their finery to show off at court; state officials had to carry with them the expenses they required for their commissions. The more eminent of these would travel in heavily protected convoys, with escorts of sufficient strength to discourage all but the most intrepid robbers. But lesser folk had to take their chance. For the trader, the merchant and the petty official, highwaymen were an occupational hazard: the businessman would build it into his selling price just as today he includes insurance among his overheads. In the 14th century Geoffrey Chaucer, performing his duties as Clerk of the Works, was robbed twice in one day between London and Eltham. Carrying ten pounds to settle some accounts, he was stopped by four men who took both his money and his horse. He returned to London to replace his losses, set out once more—and was robbed again by the same gang! As was the practice, he was at first held personally responsible, but after a while was discharged.

Occasionally the robbers' operations were conducted on a much larger scale. In 1248, at Alton on the London to Southampton road, two foreign merchants and their escort were attacked by a small army of some six hundred men—which suggests that the booty must have been well worth taking. The authorities took decisive action: many of the robbers had been identified—they included prominent local citizens and even several members of the King's Household—and eventually three hundred of the robbers were caught, convicted and hanged, while most of the others were sent to prison.

The participation of prominent citizens may seem surprising, but was not unusual. The notorious Folville gang, operating in the 1330s, was headed by Sir Eustace Folville, and it is a significant comment on the moral attitudes of the day that he was subsequently pardoned, thanks to loyal service in the Scottish Wars. Nor was his case by any means unique: the Coterel brothers were likewise pardoned and given official commissions, while other former highwaymen were actually employed to pursue rival gangs. In short, they were treated more as enemy soldiers than as enemies of society. It was a cynical but realistic attitude, given the social conditions of the day, for it was both cheaper and more effective to pardon the highwayman than to try to capture him.

The scarcity of detailed records means that we have only the most fragmentary picture of these medieval highwaymen and their way of life. But references to highwaymen in contemporary chronicles are sufficiently numerous for us to be confident that gangs of outlaws were operating in many different parts of the country throughout most of the medieval period—that they were, in fact, a permanent factor in English life, just as they were across the face of Europe where law and order were in even greater disarray. But we know very little about the outlaws themselves. We know that James Coterel and his brothers, operating in Derbyshire in the 1330s, led a gang of some twenty members but mostly worked in smaller units. We know that William Beckwith, operating in Lancashire later in the century, captained till his death in 1392 a huge gang which at times numbered as many as five hundred men. But most outlaws seem to have operated in smaller and more convenient units, if only because of the difficulty of feeding and accommodating such a large force.

Food and accommodation must have been rough and ready at the best of times. Despite the attractions of the outdoor life on a bright summer's day, existence must have been appallingly uncomfortable even by the standards of the day. However great the rewards from the robberies—and they cannot have been so very great for all but the most successful—they could not buy the pleasures of life in the towns. To eat off a stolen buck and quaff stolen wine on a warm evening in a forest hideout sounds attractive when thought of as an occasional picnic: as a day-in day-out routine the pleasure would soon pall. The sheer misery of the outlaw's life, rather than the harassment of the law, would dissuade all but the genuinely desperate.

We know that Sir Eustace Folville took to the outlaw's life because of his involvement in a vendetta-like quarrel with country neighbours. We know that he gave up the life as soon as he could secure an official pardon, choosing the soldier's life rather than the outlaw's. We know that William Beckwith became an outlaw because he had been disappointed—he would have used the word 'cheated'—in his hopes of getting an official position as forester: he captained his gang for only a short while before being killed, so we can only speculate as to what his subsequent career might have been. In most of the cases recorded by the official chronicles, outlawry seems to have been a brief interlude in an otherwise more respectable career. Was this pattern typical? What of the few 'professional' outlaws of the period, who made sufficient impact on their contemporaries for their careers to have been recounted in ballads, their deeds to have become crystallised into folklore?

Thomas Dun escapes from his pursuers—most of whom, as will be seen, are farm labourers armed with the tools of their trade.

Thomas Dun of Dunstable

Thomas Dun is supposed to have lived during the troubled reign of Henry I, in the first third of the 11th century. This would make him the earliest highwayman recorded in history, if we could be sure he existed at all.

What we are told of Dun, in accounts written long after he is supposed to have lived, contains no solid fact, just a floating mass of legend unanchored by a single corroboratable detail. He was born in Bedfordshire, near Dunstable, which lies on the very important road connecting London with the north-west of England. What his early life was, we are given no clue; the first we hear of him is his first robbery, an attack on a corn wagon on the Bedford Road. Dun got into conversation with the wagoner, then at a suitable opportunity stabbed him with a dagger. Having buried the body, he drove the wagon into town and sold it together with its contents.

This was the start of a career which lasted for twenty years, during which he was the terror of the neighbourhood. Soon he had gathered round him a band of kindred spirits, and together they comprised a force with which the local authorities could not easily deal. On one occasion the Sheriff of Bedford and a troop of armed men made a punitive attack on Dun, only to be attacked in their turn by Dun and his men—eleven of the Sheriff's men were captured and summarily hanged. Then, to add insult to injury, Dun and a group of his followers put on the dead men's clothes and, pretending to be the search party, turned up at a neighbouring castle, insisted on searching it in case the outlaws were concealed there—and took the opportunity of looting the place as they searched.

Such a tale is firmly in the heroic tradition, and so is the story that one day, learning that a party of lawyers proposed to dine at a certain inn in Bedford, Dun himself went to the inn beforehand, claiming to the landlord that he had been sent to make sure the arrangements were in hand. Then, when the lawyers arrived, he pretended to them that he was an employee of the inn. When the time came for settling the bill, he was able to exploit his ambiguous position, taking the bill to the guests as the lawyers' man, receiving the money as the landlord's man—and happily making off with it, together with the guests' hats and cloaks and the landlord's table cutlery.

How much of this is true? Little, perhaps none. Yet it is not easy to believe that such a body of legend, however spurious, could have grown up without a nucleus of truth, like the speck of grit round which the pearl is formed. Without crediting a word of the legend, I am ready to believe that there was indeed once a highway robber named Thomas Dun. But even if so, he was not so lucky in his legend as a later robber whose existence is equally dubious, but whose place in the history of outlawry is unrivalled by any man, in fact or fiction.

Robin Hood of Sherwood

In the year 1439 the respectable people of Derbyshire petitioned Parliament for help against an outlaw named Piers Venables, who had placed himself at the head of a gang of like-minded scoundrels, 'beyng of his clothinge, and in manere of insurrection wente into the wodes in that county like it hadde be Robyn Hode and his meynee'.

So in 1439 Robin Hood was already the archetype by whom other outlaws were measured. If he was not the first highwayman in history, he set the pattern. Five centuries after Piers Venables, and on the furthest side of the globe, a Transvaal horse-thief was proud to be known as 'The South African Robin Hood' and a New South Wales bushranger was given the highest accolade when he was named 'Australia's Robin Hood'. He remains the yardstick by which all his successors are judged.

Robin Hood robs a wealthy bishop not because he opposed the Church, but because he disapproved of ecclesiastics who grew fat on what they took from the common people. (Woodcut from the *Roxburghe Ballads*)

This is no mean achievement, seeing that it is far from certain whether Robin Hood lived at all; or, if he lived, when and where; or, if he really did live when and where he is said to have done, for how many of the escapades attributed to him he was really responsible. Countless scholars have contributed, and doubtless countless more will add, to the literature on Robin Hood and his Merry Men. Like Faust and Sherlock Holmes and King Arthur, he is one of the great legendary characters of mankind, and as such his career provides writers of every calibre with a happy hunting ground for conjecture and controversy.

Those who claim he never existed at all point to the fact that there is no reliable documentary evidence for his existence. Unlike the other 14th century outlaws we have already noticed, Hood's name appears in no official records, though there are some tantalising references from which the more credulous scholars have sucked what nourishment they can. The legends positively encourage this uncertainty:

> Many ane sings o' Robin Hood
> kens little where he was born.
> It wasna in the ha', the ha',
> nor in the painted bower.
> But it was in gude green-wood,
> amang the lily-flower.
>
> (*The Birth of Robin Hood*)

Those who start from the premise that he never really existed can divert themselves with all kinds of delightful theories as to why people came to believe that he *did* exist. Thus Patrick Pringle writes:

The psychology of Robin Hood is very plain. There was no Robin Hood, so it was necessary to invent one. His creation was simply a wish-fulfilment.
(*Stand and deliver*)

But that's just too glib: it may account for the popularity of Robin Hood, but it doesn't explain his creation. More sophisticated scholars can support their negative argument with more ingenious suggestions. Thus Margaret Murray, that dazzling enthusiast for the Old Religion, when Witches were priests and Kings were Divine Victims, points out that Robin is a traditional name both for the Devil and for various other pre-Christian entities, of which Robin Goodfellow is only the best known. She suggests that the name was bestowed on a wide variety of local gods, and that Robin Hood was just one of these, given a local habitation and a name and 'humanised' with legendary anecdotes. As for the 'Hood', this could either be a reference to the costume worn by the priests, or be a corruption of the phrase 'of the wood'.

It's quite fun allowing oneself to be tempted down these fascinating byways of scholarship, but they lead into labyrinths of uncertainty where you become ready to believe that anything could be true. Follow mythologist Christina Hole for instance, and in no time you'll find her, while writing of Robin Hood in her book *English Folk Heroes,* citing a certain Mr Dodsworth who quotes a Mr Long who notes that a certain Fabyan expressed the view that it was Little John, not Robin Hood, who was the dispossessed Earl of Huntingdon. The scholar Guth, on the other hand, insists that the phrase 'Earl of Huntingdon' was an ironic title bestowed on any skilled huntsman. And so the game goes on.

I do not mean to ridicule all such scholarship. It all helps us to understand the legendary aspects of the Robin Hood phenomenon. But we must remember that, no matter how many links are traced between Robin Hood and old beliefs and superstitions, they do not mean that Hood himself never existed. Personally, I find it much more probable that these folklore attributes were bestowed on a man who really did exist than that the whole Robin Hood legend is invention. Sometimes the scholars endanger their own credibility by trying to force the facts into their theories. For instance Margaret Murray, determined to include Robin Hood in her pantheon of pre-Christian nature gods, claims that he is notably anti-Christian. But this is quite simply not true: the ballads go out of their way to show him pious:

A good manner then had Robin,
in land where that he were,
every day ere he would dine
three masses would he hear.
The one in worship of the Father,
the other of the Holy Ghost,
the third was of Our dear Lady,
that he loved all the most.

(*A Lytell Geste of Robin Hood,*
printed by Wynkyn de Worde, 1495)

Well, yes, it's true that this could be a later interpolation put in by
some Christian apologist, but if you start separating out the bits that
could have been added, you'd end with nothing. What about Robin
Hood's instructions to his men:

These bishops and these archbishops,
ye shall them beat and bind;
the High Sheriff of Nottingham,
him hold ye in your mind.

Does this mean that he was against the church as a whole—or simply
against those fat clerics who abused their authority and grew rich at
the people's expense? Was he against all authority—or just the
corrupt official who held the Sheriff's post at that particular place
and time? Once again, it's a matter of deciding whether Robin Hood
was a mythical creature, who was given a human name and history
to render him believable to ordinary people, or a real man, onto
whom were grafted legendary and heroic attributes to make him a
more vivid expression of people's hopes and aspirations. If I
personally plump unhesitatingly for the second of these alternatives,
it is because I know that throughout this book we shall come across
real-life outlaws, in every period and from every culture, who have
been credited with additional virtues and feats to make them more
'heroic', and who ended by becoming almost legendary figures. If
this is known to be true in so many other cases, then, despite the lack
of evidence, I think it most likely to be true in Robin Hood's case
also.

23

If so, we may suppose that Robin Hood was a Saxon who became an outlaw, perhaps unjustly accused of some crime, but in any case having in some way run foul of the Norman establishment. On the run from the law, he gathered round him a band of men similarly circumstanced, and together they established themselves in Sherwood Forest.

Of the many stories told of him and qualities attributed to him, we need believe only what we find believable. We do not have to believe that he robbed only the rich, instructing his men:

> But look ye do no husband harm
> that tilleth with his plow.

Nor do we have to believe him as gentlemanly as the ballads suggest:

> Robin loved Our Dear Lady;
> for doubt of deadly sin
> would he no company do harm
> that woman was therein.

Yet perhaps there was some basis to these suggestions, or why else should he have been singled out above his contemporaries? As we shall see in many other instances, a little goes a long way when it's a question of generosity among brigands: the slightest concession is received with effusive gratitude by the victim. Since, like all outlaws, Robin Hood would be very dependent on the goodwill of the ordinary people among whom he lived, he would probably bestow on them a little of his plunder to retain their loyalty—just enough for people to recall:

> Christ have mercy on his soul,
> that died upon the Rood,
> for he was a good outlaw,
> and did poor men much good.

When it comes to the actual stories, fact has probably been even more liberally laced with fiction. Yet I dare say these too have a historical origin. The High Sheriff of Nottingham would have been the natural opponent of a bandit ravaging the Sherwood area, and there is no reason to reject the feud with Sir Guy of Gisborne as apocryphal simply because there is no mention of the knight in the chronicles of the day. The story is told with great circumstantial detail:

> He took Sir Guy's head by the hair,
> and sticked it on his bow's end.
> 'Thou hast been traitor all thy life,
> which thing must have an end.'
>
> Robin pulled forth an Irish knife,
> and nicked Sir Guy in the face,
> that he was never on woman born
> could tell whose head it was.
>
> (*Robin Hood and Guy of Gisborne*)

Not a scrap of this is confirmed by any official record. But there is a tradition that Robin Hood lived during the reign of a King Edward, and it is a fact that Edward II visited Yorkshire in 1323, passing through Nottinghamshire on his way, and that from March to November of the following year a certain Robert or Robin Hood was Groom of the Chambers at Court in London. This would fit in with the story that Robin Hood met the King, who pardoned him for his misdeeds (we have already noticed how willing the authorities were to pardon outlaws in order to curtail their activities) and took him back to London as a courtier. After November 1323, Robin/Robert the Groom is no longer mentioned; and this again fits in with the story that after a while Robin Hood grew weary of life at the Court, asked the King for leave of absence, and ran back to the woods and never reappeared:

> Robin dwelt in greene-wood
> twenty year and two:
> for all dread of Edward our King,
> again he would not go.

If we accept this flimsy but not improbable identification, it is interesting to note that less than forty years later Robin Hood was already a legendary figure. In Langland's *Vision of Piers Plowman,* written about 1360, a drunken priest admits that though he cannot remember the words of the Lord's Prayer, he can rhyme of Robin Hood and Randulph Earl of Chester. This suggests that a body of Robin Hood material was already circulating among the people. Before long his legend had become fused with other local traditions and I don't doubt that the mythologists are right in suggesting that the Robin Hood Games and other festivities bearing his name date back to earlier customs, quite probably associated with the pre-Christian religion of the country. There is a good story of how Bishop Latimer, coming to a country town on a holy day, decided to preach in the parish church. To his surprise he found the church closed, and was told, 'Sir, this is a busy day with us, we cannot hear you. It is Robin Hood's day, and the parish are gone abroad to gather for Robin Hood'. The Bishop was furious that irreligious customs should be preferred to church observances, and said as much in a sermon preached to young Edward VI in 1549. But when in 1555 the authorities tried to suppress the Robin Hood festivities, there were riots, and more when they tried again in 1561.

During the centuries which followed, the Robin Hood legend established itself ever more firmly, not in the least hampered by the shortage of true facts—a shortage so acute that we cannot even say whether the King was Edward II, for there are strong links with Richard I also. However, this may be simply because Richard, too, has always been a particular hero of the English who have always had a special fondness for kings who spend their reigns fighting wars in other people's countries.

There are places named for Robin Hood in Ludlow and Somerset, Yorkshire and Cumberland, in Scotland and on the outskirts of London. There is a flower named after him, and a wind, and any number of pubs. We know that he loved a suitably heroic lady named Maid Marian, though she appears in none of the oldest versions of his history, not being added until the 16th century. We know him from books and ballads, from cinema and television. It's frustrating that we know so little about him, but perhaps the truth would shatter rather too many of our fancies. Better to go on believing:

> Robin was a proud outlaw,
> the while he walked on ground.
> So courteous an outlaw as he was one
> was never none y-found.

Robin Hood, Maid Marian
and their companions enjoy
the delights of the outdoor
life. Such scenes as this
make it all look delightful:
the reality must have been a
great deal less comfortable.
(Victorian steel engraving
by Stephanoff)

Though no other medieval robber achieved a fame to compare with that of Robin Hood, the outlaw continued to menace the traveller. A few names emerge from the records. There was Henry William Genyembre, horse thief, executed at York Castle in 1585: there were Amos Lawson and Ebenezer Moor: there was Walter Tracey, executed at the age of thirty-eight, whose chief claim to fame is that he once stopped and robbed Ben Jonson the playwright. Sir John Popham, who ultimately became Lord Chief Justice, supplemented his income as a young man in the 1550s by taking purses on the highway, and only at the age of thirty or so yielded to his wife's suggestions and took up the law as both more respectable and more lucrative than highway robbery.

It was a violent, unsettled period, and England's continual involvement in foreign wars did not increase stability. In his book of Worthies, Thomas Fuller looked back from 1640 to this earlier period:

The land then swarmed with people who had been soldiers, who had never gotten (or else quite forgotten) any other vocation. Hard it was for Peace to feed all the idle mouths which a former War did breed.

Typical of these rootless soldiers was Gamaliel Ratsey, of Market Deeping in Lincolnshire, a man of respectable parentage and good education who had served in the army in Ireland. On his return he found himself unable to settle to any honest occupation, took to robbery and subsequently to a highwayman's career. When he was caught and executed at Bedford, in March 1605, his biography was published and many stories were attributed to him which were to become standard items in the lives of later highwaymen. There was the time he stopped a Cambridge scholar and forced him to deliver a learned discourse: and the occasion when he stopped an actor and required him to recite a speech from *Hamlet*. Similar anecdotes were to be told of later highwaymen, and perhaps Ratsey's biographer lifted them from an earlier outlaw: but the 'Hamlet' touch is a shrewd one, for the play only appeared in 1602.

Two years before Ratsey was executed was born one of the few highwaymen ever to be caught and yet escape the hangman's noose. John Clavel was the son of a respectable Dorset squire, who took to highway robbery for reasons unknown. Though an amateur, he very quickly made a reputation for himself, but was caught in 1626. A contemporary news-letter informs us:

February 11th, Mr Clavell, a gentleman, a knight's eldest son, a great highway robber, and of posts, was, together with a soldier, his companion, arraigned and condemned, on Monday last, at the King's Bench bar. He

John Clavel, the repentant highwayman whose display of penitence saved the neck beneath that fancy collar.

That I may neither beare anothers blame
Through wronge suspicions nor yet act ye same
At any time hereafter, but prove true
Loe to be knowne you haue my face at viewe

pleaded for himself that he had never struck or wounded any man, had never taken anything from their bodies, as rings, etc., never cut their girths or saddles, or done them, when he robbed, any corporeal violence. He was, with his companion, reprieved.

Having won his reprieve, he then tried for a complete release, and with this in mind composed his *Recantation of an Ill-led Life* in which he confesses his crimes but pleads for mercy. In the course of the book, which is chiefly in verse, he proves his sincerity by giving travellers helpful advice:

> Next, of a Thief the usual marks are these
> (which as you ride you may observe with ease):
> they muffle with their cloaks, or else their coat
> hides all their clothes, that so you may not note
> what suits they have. A handkerchief they wear
> about their necks, or Cipress, which they rear
> over their mouths, and noses, with their hand
> just at the time when as they bid you stand.

Great poetry it is not, but perhaps its very awkwardness gave credit to his good intentions. At any rate, his recantation had the desired effect and Clavel was released to die a free man a quarter of a century later. By the time of his death in 1642, the history of England was taking a course which was to bring about, as a by-product, the greatest age of the English highwayman.

3 'The highway is my hope'

Stop, Stop's the word all dread to hear,
    your gold and your gems resign,
when my pistol's cocked and my look's severe —
    for a desperate life is mine!
How ladies scream, how with rage men glow,
    while their purses I unload!
Then I cry Good Night, with a smile and a bow,
    And Hurrah! Hurrah! for the road!

(*Paul Clifford*)

Suddenly, in the middle of the 17th century, Englishmen, so accustomed to fighting the French or the Spanish or the Dutch, and if need be the Welsh and the Scots, found themselves fighting other Englishmen. After a century and a half of peace and stability, war was again abroad in England.

Amazingly, England's machinery of government survived. The only issue was who should control that machinery, and for the moment that was settled when one party cut off the head of the other party's leader. Thanks to this decisive step, the effects of the English Civil War were nowhere near as horrific as those of the Religious Wars in contemporary France or the Thirty Years War in Germany, where, outside the security of the towns, there was virtually no such thing as law and order, and the peasantry were in a permanent state of war against bandit gangs largely composed of out-of-work soldiers.

But even in England conditions were bad enough. Bitterness and divisions appeared that were to take generations to heal. And in England, too, it was the former soldier who took to highway robbery as his only recourse. Mostly, of course, royalist soldiers—those who had fought on the losing side and who now, with their king decapitated and his heir in foreign exile, found it hard to find a place under the new regime.

Not every highwayman of the later 17th century was a royalist soldier, but the battlefields of Naseby and Marston Moor were the training grounds of many who now took to demanding a living from society by force of arms. During the immediate post-war period the problem became so serious that General Fairfax in September 1649 proclaimed that the army was to take part in the suppression of highwaymen. Thanks to his offer of a reward of ten pounds a man, a good number had been caught and executed by Christmas.

But not all were deterred: a tract of the day vaunted the highwayman's motives:

> To beg is base, as base to pick a purse;
> to cheat, more base of all theft—that is worse.
> Nor beg nor cheat will I—I scorn the same;
> but while I live, maintain a soldier's name.
> I'll purse it, I: the Highway is my Hope!
> His heart's not great that fears a little rope.

> (*The Cashiered Soldier*)

So even at this early date we find it implied that there is a nobility about the highwayman's career which raises it above other forms of robbery, and that robbery is itself nobler than other forms of crime. To take away from other men what they have earned with hard days of honest work may be a base thing to do, but if you have no choice, then this is the least base way of going about it. And for the landless, jobless ex-royalist in the 1650s, it must really have seemed that he had no choice.

The Cavalier Tradition

The English Highwayman enjoyed a reputation for courtesy and chivalry which amazed foreign visitors to the country. The German traveller von Archenholz noted with wonder:

They assure you they are very sorry that poverty has driven them to that shameful recourse, and end by demanding your purse in the most courteous manner.

It was a reputation which survived even when individual Highwaymen failed to maintain the code. Most Highwaymen were, in truth, of humble origins, yet they were apt to put on airs when they took to the road. They felt they had a model to live up to. As Highwaymen, they claimed the respect of others, and a good many of them were willing so to conduct themselves as to earn that respect.

Because they were robbers by necessity rather than by upbringing, the cavalier Highwaymen came to their job with an amateur insouciance and grace, and thus unwittingly set the pattern for their successors. In a short time a tradition had been established. Perhaps it was only a small minority who really followed the tradition, but they were the ones who caught the popular imagination.

In June 1652 the diarist John Evelyn had an encounter with some Highwaymen:

The weather being hot, and having sent my man on before, I rode negligently under favour of the shade, till within three miles of Bromley two cut-throats started out, and striking with long staves at the horse and taking hold of the reins, threw me down, took my sword, and haled me into a deep thicket some quarter of a mile from the highway, where they might securely rob me, as they soon did. What they got of money was not considerable, but they took two rings, the one an emerald with diamonds, the other an onyx, and a pair of buckles set with rubies and diamonds, which were of value, and after all bound my hands behind me and my feet, having before pulled off my boots; they then set me up against an oak, with most bloody threats to cut my throat if I offered to cry out or make any noise, for they should be within hearing, I not being the person they looked for. I told them if they had not basely surprised me they should not have had so easy a prize, and that it would teach me never to ride near an hedge, since had I been in the mid-way they durst not have adventured on me: at which they cocked their pistols, and told me they had long guns too, and were 14 companions . . . My horse's bridle they slipped, and searched the saddle, which they pulled off, but let the horse graze, and then turning again bridled him and tied him to a tree, yet so as he might graze, and thus left me bound. My horse was perhaps not taken because he was marked and cropped on both ears, and well known on that road. Left in this manner grievously was I tormented with flies, ants, and the sun, nor was my anxiety little how I should get loose in that solitary place, where I could neither hear or see any creature but my poor horse and a few sheep straggling in the copse. After near two hours attempting, I got my hands to turn palm to palm, having been tied back to back, and then it was long before I could slip the cord over my wrists to my thumb, which I at last did, and then soon unbound my feet, and saddling my horse and roaming awhile about I at last perceived dust to rise, and soon after heard the rattling of a cart, towards which I made, and by the help of two country men I got back into the highway. I rode to Colonel Blount's, a great justiciary of the times, who sent out hue and cry immediately. The next morning, sore as my wrists and arms were, I went to London and got 500 tickets printed and dispersed by an officer of Goldsmiths' Hall, and within 2 days had tidings of all I had lost except my sword which had a silver hilt, and some trifles . . . Thus did God deliver me from these villains.

John Evelyn's encounter, sufficiently dramatic though it must have seemed to him, is matter-of-fact when set beside the picturesque tales of the famous Highwaymen of the period, but his experience is probably the more typical. Most Highwaymen must have been the simple ruffians such a way of life would be expected to attract: those who self-consciously modelled themselves on the leaders of their profession—as did James Maclean and Jack Rann in the next century—were the exceptions rather than the rule.

It would be a thankless task to present the highwayman as he really was: a fellow rarely heroic, generally foul-mouthed and cruel, and often cowardly. No novelist would be likely to thank the frank historian for this disservice; and I do not think the historian who came to the subject in this cold scientific spirit of a demonstrator would be widely read. Most of us like to keep a few of the illusions we believed in when schoolboys. To abolish the traditional courtesy of Claude Du Vall or the considerate conduct of Captain Hind would be strokes of the unkindest.

Charles G. Harper, Half Hours with the Highwaymen, 1908

Harper was writing in an age which had only just begun to appreciate the significance of legend. If he shrank from revealing the Highwayman in all his ignobility, it was because he didn't want to spoil a good story. Today we have learned that legend has a value *because* it is legend, and known to be legend. If people have made Highwaymen into Heroes, it isn't simply for love of a good story: deeper instincts are at work.

And those instincts are related to those which established the English Highwayman tradition in the first place. When a man opted for the Highwayman's life, he recognised to himself that he was crossing a social boundary, promoting himself into the officer class. Like a cricketer, even though he might be by birth one of the 'Players', he could learn to conduct himself as did the 'Gentlemen'. Although he might not always keep to them, he was aware of the unwritten rules: even if he did not scrupulously observe it, he recognised the existence of a code of conduct.

So the archetypal Highwayman emerges cast in the traditional Cavalier mould. He wears a plumed, broad-brimmed hat aslant over his long and curly hair. His moustache is splendid, his beard a replica of his beheaded king's. In his spare moments he finds time to write delightful verses to blushing Lucastas and ringletted Lucindas, but most of the time he is dashing about on his horse, crying 'For God and King!' and behaving gallantly on all occasions. Compared with him, what a dull dog is Cromwell's Ironside. Crop-haired, dressed in drab grey or puritanical black, unsmilingly opposed to dancing and playacting and only too prone to chop down maypoles, preferring sermons to sonnets and more likely to be named Praise-God Barebones than Prince Rupert of the Rhine—such a man may win battles, but not hearts or imaginations!

Of course the storybook Cavalier never existed in fact. It was a rough and violent age, and even the most sophisticated lived lives of a coarseness and crudity which would appall us today. 'You whining bitch, how you throw your snot and snivel about for nothing at all!' complained the Highwayman Bob Congden when a lady's maid proved reluctant to part with her savings: yet he was a graduate of Cambridge University. Jacob Halsey, having robbed a fair victim of her material possessions, demanded a further prize in words whose studied elegance only cloaks the viciousness beneath: 'My pretty lamb, an insurrection of an unruly member obliges me to make use of you on an extraordinary occasion; therefore I must dismount thy alluring body, to the end I may come into thee.'

The record of violence is a full one. Captain Evan Evans mercilessly thrashed a man for having no more than fivepence upon him. Gilder Roy, a Scottish Highwayman of good family, meeting with resistance from a judge and his servants, stripped the coachman and the two footmen naked, tied them up and threw them into a pond to drown, shot the horses, and hanged the judge. Thomas Wilmot cut off the finger of a woman to obtain her ring. William Cady, when a victim swallowed her wedding ring in order to preserve it, shot her and cut her open. John Withers, having forgotten to put on his mask and fearing that his victim might identify him, cut his throat, slit open his stomach, filled it with stones and threw the body into a stream.

None of which is the kind of conduct we expect from the gallant Highwayman of legend.

Captain James Hind

If one man more than any other set the style for the Highwayman's profession, it was James Hind, the best known highway robber of his day and hero of contemporary verses a cut above the normal level of ballad doggerel:

The True Portraiture of
Captain James Hind.
(Woodcut of 1652)

The true Por
traiture of Captain
JAMES HIND,
the Robber, who
died for Treaſon.

He made our wealth one common store,
he robbed the rich to feed the poor:
what did immortal Caesar more?

If in due light his deeds we scan
as Nature points us out the plan,
Hind was an honourable man!

Honour, the virtue of the brave,
to Hind that turn of genius gave
which made him scorn to be a slave.

Born at Chipping Norton in 1616, the son of a saddler, Hind was
apprenticed as a boy to a butcher, but didn't care for the trade,
borrowed two pounds from his mother and ran off to London. There,
at the tender age of fifteen, he quickly acquired a taste for the
pleasures of the town, drinking, whoring, and scraping by as best he

35

could. Inevitably he took to crime, and no less inevitably was caught: in the Poultry Compter prison he met a thief named Thomas Allen who invited him, on his release, to join his gang of highway robbers. He was taken to Shooter's Hill, Blackheath, for a trial: alone, Hind stopped a traveller on the Dover Road, relieved him of fifteen pounds, then seeing that he had left him penniless, gave him back one pound saying 'This is for handsel sake.' 'Which generosity,' his contemporary biographer commented, 'made Tom Allen very proud, to see his comrade rob a Person with a Good Grace'.

Hind quickly established a reputation for politeness, courtesy and consideration. Happening to be in Warwick, he saw a commotion outside an inn, and found that a merciless money-lender was distraining on the landlord. Hind, who perhaps knew the innkeeper, paid the debt for him; then he waited for the money-lender outside the town gates and took the money back, with twenty pounds more as interest. When the money-lender tried to reclaim his losses from the innkeeper, his victim was able to produce a signed receipt. Similar stories were told of many subsequent Highwaymen—I like to think that in Hind's case at least, it was not an invention.

Many of the feats attributed to Hind, as with other Highwaymen of the period, consist of attacks made on leaders of the Parliamentary Party. Thus General Fairfax is supposed to have been robbed by Mary Frith whom we shall be meeting later, and Lady Fairfax was robbed once by John Cottington and again by Zachary Howard, who also ravished both her and her daughter ('beginning,' we are informed, 'with the daughter'). Two Highwaymen tried to rob Oliver Cromwell himself, both unsuccessfully—one was Cottington again, the other was Captain Hind, who with his confederate Allen staged a large attack on the Protector's carriage. The escort proved too strong for them, however, and several of the robbers were captured, including Allen who was duly hanged. Hind is also supposed to have stopped the prominent Puritan leader Hugh Peters, with whom he carried on a lengthy theological discussion before robbing him of his worldly goods.

So well known did Hind become that a play based on his career was actually staged in 1651, while he was still active. At this time he was combining his career on the roads with political activities in the Royalist cause: he had fought for the King at the Battle of Worcester, had escaped from the Siege of Colchester in 1648, disguised as a sailor, say some accounts, or as a woman, say others. In 1649 he had been with the future Charles II in The Hague, and then his political activities took him to Ireland, where he was wounded at Youghal, and subsequently to the Scilly Isles.

Yet even while out of England, he was credited with many of the robberies that took place. In September 1649 a newspaper published this item:

Last night was brought into this gaol (Bedford) two prisoners taken up upon pursuit by the county, for robbing some soldiers of about £300 upon the way, in the day-time; there were five in the fact, and are very handsome gentlemen; they will not confess their names, and therefore are supposed to be gentlemen of quality, and 'tis conceived they are of the knot of Captain Hind, that grand thief of England, that hath his associates upon all roads. They strewd at least £100 upon the way, to keep the pursuers doing, that they might not follow them.

It seems likely that Hind was in fact in the Scilly Isles at that time, but the device of scattering some of their loot to slow down the pursuers is very much Hind's style: much of his success was due to his ability to think big. He advised his colleagues, 'Disgrace not yourselves for small sums, but aim high, and for great ones: the least will bring you to the gallows.'

What brought Hind to the gallows was an unfortunate chapter of accidents. Although his career was notable for his distaste for violence, there had been one tragic episode at Knole, Berkshire. When making his escape after a robbery, noticing a horseman coming up behind him, he took him to be a pursuer, and turned and shot him. Unfortunately, he turned out to be George Sympson, a gentleman's servant, who had no connection with the affair. Some time later, in London, Hind was recognised by someone who had been involved in the matter and he was arrested, charged and taken to Reading to stand trial. Just at this time an Act of Oblivion was passed, granting amnesty to all prisoners as part of a campaign to restore social stability after the Civil War. Hind would have been released, but the authorities switched the charge to one of treason and sent him to Worcester to stand trial for his political activities. There was no oblivion for treason, and, on September 24th 1652, he was hanged and quartered. His head was placed on the Severn Bridge and other portions of his anatomy displayed at the various gates of the city. He died true to his political convictions:

At the place of execution he confessed that most of the Robberies which he ever committed, were upon the Republican Party, of whose principles he had such an abhorrence that nothing troubled him so much as to die before he saw his Royal Master established in his Throne.

Captain Philip Stafford

Captain Stafford was another Royalist who suffered for having fought too conspicuously on behalf of the King. Born about 1622, the son of a gentleman farmer near Newbury, he had his estates sequestered after the war when many such reprisals were being taken by the victorious Parliamentarians. Stafford saw no other course but to rob the society which had robbed him, and in a short while he was one of the most notorious Highwaymen operating in that favourite haunt of robbers, Maidenhead Thicket on the main road from London to the South-West. His exploits were not especially dramatic: we are told, for instance, of how he stopped a clergyman, stole his horse and forty guineas, and left him tied to a tree just as John Evelyn had been left; but by such means he gradually acquired sufficient funds to retire back into respectable life.

He chose a village in the North of England, and lived there quietly for a while. In course of time he was appointed minister and became noted for his preaching. But after the excitements of his early career, respectable life was too humdrum, so one day he left his ministry and the village and came south again, bringing the church plate with him.

Once again he chose the Reading neighbourhood as his scene of operations: but he was able to carry out only one hold-up. Meeting a farmer returning from market with thirty-three pounds for wheat he had sold, he took it off him and rode on. Two gentlemen overtook the farmer and heard his story: they rode in pursuit of Stafford, no doubt with a reward in mind, came up with him, forced him to dismount, regained the money and took him to the magistrate. At the next Assizes Stafford was of course found guilty and sentenced. While waiting for his execution he lived very comfortably in Reading Gaol, being visited by many of his old comrades-in-arms. Some of these formed plans to spring him, but news came to the prison governor and the execution date was brought forward. After being hanged, he was buried in St Mary's Churchyard.

Mary Frith

Highwaywomen are almost non-existent in the history of the subject. Many highwaymen had female associates, but only rarely did they take any active part in the robberies. Mary Frith was one of the few who went into the business on her own account, though even in her case it was only a brief interlude between other and more certain ways of making a dishonest living.

Born in 1584, she went into domestic service as a girl, and hated it. But what alternative ways of life were open to her? Even her

The Roaring Girle.

OR
Moll Cut-Purse.

As it hath lately beene Acted on the Fortune-stage by
the Prince his Players.

Written by *T. Middleton* and *T. Dekkar*.

My case is alter'd, I must worke for my liuing.

Printed at *London* for *Thomas Archer*, and are to be sold at his
shop in Popes head-pallace, neere the Royall
Exchange. 1611.

admiring biographer had to admit that she was physically
unpreposessing:

She was not meant for the pleasure or delight of man. A very tomrig or
rumpscuttle he was, and delighted and sported only in boys' play and
practice.

Her portraits bear this verdict out, and incidentally generally depict
her with a pipe in her mouth. Her biographer tells us, 'In her time,
tobacco being grown a great mode, she was mightily took with the
pastime of smoking.'

It was no doubt her male companions who encouraged her to take
to crime: she quickly became a skilled pickpocket, and earned the
nickname of 'Moll Cutpurse' by which she became so well known
that Middleton and Dekker wrote a play, *The Roaring Girl*,
supposedly based on her criminal career. After a few years of
thieving she shrewdly saw that fencing is a more profitable side of

39

the business than the actual thieving, and she was soon established as one of the most successful receivers of stolen goods in London.

Somehow she managed to avoid the law, but during the Civil War and Commonwealth period her fortunes declined, and she resolved to supplement her income with a little thieving. But, whether because she had lost her old skill, or because she was too well-known in the streets of London, or simply because she was after larger profits, picking pockets was not her game this time. Instead, perhaps inspired by the lucrative exploits of Hind and Stafford, she resolved to try her hand at highway robbery. She proved as successful in this as in her other enterprises: quite early in her career she held up General Fairfax and two servants single-handed on Hounslow Heath; having shown that she meant business by killing the servants' horses and wounding the General in the arm when he tried to reach for a weapon, she took £250 off him.

But her highway career was not to be long-lived. Soon after this she was captured, and found herself in prison for the first time in her life: though it was no error on her part that brought her to Newgate, but the fact that her horse failed her at Turnham Green while trying to evade pursuers—the sort of thing that might happen to anyone.

But though she found her way to Newgate Prison, she managed not to continue the traditional road farther, from Newgate to the scaffold at Tyburn. Though shortage of funds had inspired her to take to the highway, she was not without resources and was able to gather together £2000—an enormous sum at that period—to purchase her release. Whether she continued her criminal career after her release, history does not record, though it is doubtful whether she tried her luck on the roads again—she was, after all, some sixty years old by now! All we know is that she died in 1659, too soon by a year to witness the restoration of the monarchy—an event she so confidently expected that she left £20 in her will that her heirs might celebrate it in appropriate fashion.

John Cottington (known as 'Mull'd Sack')

Cottington was the youngest of the nineteen shildren of a drunken haberdasher of Cheapside, who died in poverty soon after John was born in 1611. As a boy he was apprenticed as a chimney sweep, but ran away at the age of thirteen and took to petty thieving. He must have had a flair for it, for it was said of his success as a pickpocket that he stole 'almost enough to have built Saint Paul's Cathedral'. During the Civil War he fought, inevitably, on the King's side and, after the fighting, returned to thieving. One of his most picturesque

John Cottington, known as Mulled Sack. (Copperplate from Caulfield's *Wonderful Characters*)

40

MULLD·SAKE

I Walke the Strand, and Westminster, and Scorne
to march i'th Cittie; though I beare the Horne,
My Feather, and my yellow Band, accord
to prove me Courtier, My Boote, Spur and Sword,

My smoking Pipe, Scarfe, Garter, Rose on Shoe,
Showe my brave mind, t'affect what Gallants do.
I Singe dance drinke and merrily pass the day,
and like a Chimney, sweeps all care away.

pub.d Aug.t 28.th 1794 by Caulfield and Herbert.

exploits was his robbery of Lady Fairfax, wife of the General, when she arrived to attend a service at St Martin's Church, Ludgate. Cottington's associates neatly removed the axle pin so that the carriage collapsed. Cottington, dressed as a gentleman, stepped forward as though to help, then swiftly cut her watch chain with his scissors and took also a handsome gold watch set with diamonds.

Not all his attempts were so successful. An attack on Cromwell himself was nearly disastrous—his colleague, Captain Horne, was caught and hanged, and the same fate nearly overtook Cottington. Much the same happened when, with another Highwayman named Tom Cheney, they rashly attacked a Parliamentary officer, Colonel Hewson, on Hounslow Heath within sight of his own men. The Colonel's men gave chase, and Cheney was caught and executed. Once again Cottington escaped.

Like other former Royalist soldiers, he claimed to be carrying on something like a guerilla war on behalf of the King's cause, with the implication that the robberies had a military rather than a purely private purpose. Thus, when he stopped an Army pay wagon, carrying £4,000 for the Gloucester garrison, as it slowly climbed Shotover Hill, near Oxford, he justified his action in these words:

This that I have taken, is as much mine as theirs who own it, being all extorted from the Public by the rapacious Members of our Commonwealth to enrich themselves, maintain their Janizaries, and keep honest people in subjection.

He lived constantly on the edge of disaster. He was arrested on suspicion of the pay wagon robbery, but the prosecution failed to muster sufficient evidence. Soon after this, having accidentally killed a man in the course of a robbery, he fled to the continent and made his way to the court of Charles Stuart at Cologne. Here, instead of attaching himself to the future King's entourage, he took the chance to steal some silver plate to the value of £1,500, and made his way back to England. Soon after this he was arrested and convicted. He tried to purchase a reprieve by offering information about Charles' intentions, but could come up with nothing worthwhile. He was hanged at Smithfield Rounds in 1656, at the age of forty-five. His nickname of 'Mull'd Sack' was derived from his favourite beverage when he was in funds, and which must have been a welcome restorative after a cold night on the Road.

Claude Duval

Virtually every Highwayman who made a success of his career on the English roads was himself an Englishman: and most of the rest were Irishmen. Claude Duval was one of the very few complete foreigners, having been born in 1643 at Domfront in Normandy: his father was a miller, his mother the daughter of a tailor. He left home at the age of thirteen or fourteen and made his way to Paris where he took service with an exiled English Royalist, and with whom he travelled to England at the restoration of Charles II in 1660.

He very soon left this employment and took to crime, operating on Hounslow Heath and Blackheath for preference. He quickly made so big a name for himself that he headed a list of Highwaymen published in the *London Gazette*. By the time of his most celebrated exploit, he was evidently the leader of a gang:

He, with his Squadron, overtakes a Coach, having intelligence of a booty of £400 in it. In the Coach was a knight, his lady, and only one serving-maid, who, perceiving five horsemen making up to them, presently imagined that they were beset; and they were confirmed in this apprehension by seeing them whisper to one another, and ride backwards and forwards. The lady, to show that she was not afraid, takes a Flageolet out of her pocket and plays. Duval takes the hint, plays also, and excellently well, upon a Flageolet of his own, and in this posture he rides up to the coachside.

'Sir,' says he to the person in the coach, 'your Lady plays excellently, and I doubt not but that she dances as well. Will you please to walk out of the coach and let me have the honour to dance one Coranto with her upon the Heath?'

'Sir,' said the person in the coach, 'I dare not deny anything to one of your quality and good mind. You seem a Gentleman, and your request is very reasonable.'

Which said, the lackey opens the boot, out comes the Knight, Duval leaps lightly off his horse and hands the Lady out of the coach. They danced, and here it was that Duval performed marvels; the best masters in London, except those that are French, not being able to show such footing as he did in his great French riding boots.

The dancing being over (there being no violins, Duval sung the Coranto himself) he waits on the Lady to her coach. As the Knight was going in, says Duval to him, 'Sir, you have forgot to pay the Musick.' 'No, I have not,' replied the Knight, and putting a hand under the seat, pulls out a £100 in a bag, and delivers it to him, which Duval took with a very good grace.

Memoirs of Monsieur Du Vall, 1670

Such courteous behaviour earned him a special reputation, until any robbery in which politeness was displayed came to be credited to him. Thus a newsletter of 1666 reports:

Last Monday week in Holborn Fields, while several gentlemen were travelling to Newmarket to the races there, a Highwayman very politely begged their purses, for he said he was advised that he should win a great sum if he adventured some guineas with the Competers at Newmarket on a

Claude Duval invites his victim to dance a coranto on the road. (Engraved from the painting by Frith.

certain horse called 'Bo-Peep', which my Lord Exeter was to run a match. He was so pressing that they resigned their money to his keeping (not without sight of his pistols), he telling them that, if they would give him their names and the names of the places where they might be found, he would return to them that had lent, at usury. It is thought that his venture was not favourable, for the Gentlemen have not received neither principal nor interest. It is thought that it was Monsieur Claude Duval, or one of his knot, that ventured the Gentlemen's money for them.

Sometime in the mid-1660s, perhaps finding things getting too hot for comfort in England, he returned to France to try his luck there. He got involved with a gentleman to whom he pretended to be an alchemist, and managed to get away with his patron's money, but he found highway robbery in France not nearly so lucrative. His biographer comments:

In truth, the air of France is not good for persons of his constitution, it being the custom there to travel in great companies, well armed, and with little money. The danger of being resisted, and the danger of being taken, are much greater there: and the quarry much less than in England. And if, by chance, a dapper fellow, with fine black eyes, and a white peruke be taken there, and found guilty of robbing, all the women in the town don't presently take the alarm, and run to the King to beg his life.

That passage was of course written after Duval's life, and the reference is to what did in fact happen in England when he was finally captured, while drunk, at the Hole-in-the-Wall Tavern, in Chandos Street near Covent Garden. So great was his reputation, that vigorous efforts were made to win a reprieve for him, but his guilt was too notorious. He was duly hanged on 21 January, 1670. After the execution, his body was displayed in state at the Tangier Tavern, St Giles, in a room draped in black and hung with funeral escutcheons. Candles burned, cloaked men kept watch; many fashionable ladies came to witness the spectacle, masked but with tears running down their cheeks. The Judge who had sentenced Duval called the exhibition scandalous and had it closed down; none the less Duval received a splendid funeral at St Paul's Church, Covent Garden, where he was buried beneath this epitaph:

> Here lies Duval. Reader, if Male thou art,
> Look to thy purse: if female, to thy heart.
> Much havoc has he made of both, for all
> Men he made stand, and women he made fall.
> The second Conqueror of the Norman race,
> Knights to his arms did yield, and Ladies to his face.

> Old Tyburn's Glory: England's illustrious thief,
> Duval, the Ladies' joy; Duval, the Ladies' grief.

Francis Jackson

Jackson was not a distinguished thief: after a short and inglorious career he was caught, condemned, sentenced and executed. What makes him of special interest is the fact that while he was hanging in chains at Hampstead in 1674, there was published a book which he had written while awaiting execution in prison.

First, Jackson tells us a little about his life as a Highwayman. His description of a typical robbery puts a little flesh onto the bare bones of most such narrative:

> We were four in company, and took our road towards Maidenhead, more for intelligence' sake than for any present booty. In Maidenhead we dined, and towards four oclock in summer time we travelled on for Reading, making a little halt by the way at Maidenhead Thicket, expecting there to light upon some prize. Having waited an hour or more to no purpose, we proposed to distribute ourselves, and rode into Reading singly, and that two should lie in one inn, and two in the other, for the better benefit of observation . . . After supper we heard what our hearts desired.

What Jackson heard was that an attorney would be travelling next morning along a particular road, with 150 guineas in a secret hiding place in his saddle. Jackson made some excuse to leave the inn and passed the information to his confederates at the other inn. Next morning they lay in wait for the attorney and robbed him, surprising him by their knowledge of his secret cache.

As might be expected in a prison confession, Jackson belittles the Highwayman and his trade:

> Highwaymen for the most part are such, who never were acquainted with an honest trade, whom either want of money or employment prompted them to undertake these dangerous designs. To make their persons appear more formidable, and to gain respect, they dub one another Colonel, Major, or at least a Captain, who never arrived to a greater height than a trooper disbanded, or at the utmost a lifeguardsman cashiered for misdemeanour.

A good part of his book amounts to a veritable do-it-yourself manual, with the supposed intention of warning the traveller but at the same time giving many useful hints to novices in the art of highway robbery. He tells us how a Highwayman should try to plead affectingly at his trial; why he should be loyal to his colleagues, so that they may be loyal to him if need be; stresses the importance of training; explains the various ways of getting information about worthwhile prey. He describes disguises—beards and wigs to conceal the appearance; a pebble in the mouth to make the voice unrecognizable; he advises each member of the gang to adopt a *nom de guerre* so that the victims shall not recall any genuine names called out in the heat of the action.

All this, of course, purports to be a warning to the public of the tricks that the Highwaymen are liable to get up to, but it is impossible to say in what spirit Jackson was writing. Certainly he is generous in his advice to the traveller, how to take the best precautions against being robbed. He advises travellers to travel in pairs, neither singly nor in a bunch: thus if one pair are ambushed, their companions riding at a distance can either come to their assistance or give the alarm. He has advice for innkeepers, too: they can readily spot the Highwayman by his habit of lounging casually at the window, watching the road—for what he is really doing is sizing up the passing traffic to see whether any likely looking prey offers itself. (Jackson recognises, however, that innkeepers are frequently in league with the Highwaymen, and advises his robbers to cultivate the landlord's company, and patronise him generously, as a source of valuable information.)

And then, every now and again in the course of his composition, the author seems to recollect where he is and what is going to happen to him, and remembers that he has a moral duty to perform. Regretfully, resignedly, he observes:

All the time they can spare from robbing and undoing poor harmless men, is spent in wine and women: so that the sunshine of their prosperity lasts but a moment, not so long as to warm their hands by the blazing fire of their prodigality, before cold death comes and seizeth them.

John Nevison

Described as already a 'ringleader in rudeness and debauchery' at the age of fourteen, it is not surprising that John Nevison, though born in 1639 of respectable parents at Pontefract, began his career by stealing his father's money and his schoolmaster's horse, and making his way to London. Prudently, he killed the horse on the outskirts of London, so leaving no traces for any pursuers.

For the next three years he seems to have lived more or less honestly, working for a brewer, then he seized his opportunity, stole £300 from his employer and fled to the Continent. He met a Dutch girl and persuaded her to elope with him, bringing her father's money and jewelry. He then deserted her and joined the British army fighting in Flanders. The military life suited him no better than married life so he deserted once again and returned to England, where he became a Highwayman. Before long he had built himself a reputation comparable to Duval's, being particularly courteous to women: 'in all his exploits, Nevison was tender to the fair sex, and bountiful to the poor. He was also a true Royalist, and never levied any contributions upon the Royalists.'

When he was still only twenty-one years old, he had acquired a fortune, and was able to revisit his father's home in the character of a gentleman, giving every indication of being frugal and industrious. He stayed with his father until the old man died. Then he seems to have organised a kind of protection racket on the drovers travelling the roads near Pontefract, levying a quarterly toll on them in return for his protection against any other thieves. So prevalent was highway robbery during this period that a good many carriers considered Nevison's proposal as a good bargain.

But Nevison had not given up robbery in its more customary form, and it was after one such affair that he performed the exploit which was to bring him lasting fame. He had robbed a traveller on Gad's Hill, near Rochester in Kent, and was particularly anxious not to be identified by his victim. He determined to establish an alibi by riding so great a distance that it would seem impossible for him to have committed the robbery. This was the celebrated 230-mile ride to York, later credited to Dick Turpin without the slightest show of reason. At York that same evening, Nevison selected the bowling green as a suitable public place to establish his presence, and was fortunate enough to meet no less a person than the Mayor of York, who could testify to his being there. So, when in due course the Highwayman was brought into court and confronted with his victim, he was able to produce witnesses whose unshakeable testimony seemed convincing proof of Nevison's innocence.

The facts of Nevison's celebrated ride have been repeatedly disputed, including the very question of whether it really occurred at all. However, the accounts are circumstantial enough, including the attractive postscript to the effect that King Charles II, on being told of the exploit, asked to meet Nevison, christened him 'Swift Nicks', and bestowed a royal pardon on him.

Back on his own home ground of Yorkshire, he continued his career, but now there was so attractive a reward for his capture that he had to reckon not only with his victims and the officers of the law but also with amateur thief-takers. In 1684 he was beset by two brothers named Fletcher, butchers, near Howley Hall, Morley. He escaped only by shooting one of them dead. This caused the efforts to take him to be stepped up, and a few months later he was finally arrested at the Three Houses Inn at Sandal, near Wakefield in Yorkshire. He was found guilty of murder and hanged at Knavesmire on 4 May 1685, aged forty-five.

> Did you ever hear tell of that hero,
>   Bold Nevison that was his name?
> He rode about like a bold hero,
>   And with that he gained great fame.
>
> He maintained himself like a gentleman,
>   Besides, he was good to the poor.
> He rode about like a bold hero,
>   And he gained himself favour therefore.
>
> Tis now before my lord judge,
>   Oh! guilty or not do you plead?
> He smiled unto the judge and the jury,
>   And these were the words that he said:
>
> It's when that I rode on the highway,
>   I've always had money in store,
> And whatever I took from the rich,
>   I freely gave to the poor.

William Davis

Davis is an exception to most of the rules governing the Highwayman's career, and most especially that which says the Highwayman's career shall be a short one. Davis worked successfully on the Road for more than forty years before destiny finally caught up with him. Born in Wrexham about 1625, he moved to Sudbury in Gloucestershire where he married an innkeeper's daughter and eventually had eighteen children by her. By day he worked as farmer, and all the neighbourhood could witness to his prosperity but when they nicknamed him 'The Golden Farmer' because of his partiality for always settling his bills with gold, they little suspected where the gold came from.

It could be that his success in avoiding capture was due in part to the fact that he generally worked alone. He also seems to have

William Davis, the Golden Farmer, robs a traveller. (Wood engraving from Johnson's *Lives of the Highwaymen*)

displayed a notable coolness in his work, as appears in two stories from his biography:

One day, meeting three or four Stage-Coaches going to Salisbury, he stopped one of them, which was full of gentlewomen, one of which was a Quaker. All of 'em satisfied the Golden Farmer's desire, excepting this Precisian, with whom he held a long argument to no purpose; for, upon her solemn vow and asseveration, she told him she had no money, nor anything valuable about her. Whereupon, fearing he should lose the booty of the other coaches, he told her he would go and see what they had to afford him, and he would wait on her again. So having robbed the other three coaches, he returned according to his word, and the Quaker persisting still in her old tone of having nothing for him, it put the Golden Farmer into a rage, and taking hold of her shoulder, shaking her as a mastiff does a bull, he cried, 'You canting Bitch, if you dally with me at this rate, you'll certainly provoke my Spirit to be damnable rude with you: you see these good women here were so tender-hearted as to be charitable to me, and you, you whimpering whore, are so covetous as to lose your life for the sake of Mammon. Come, come, you hollow Bitch, open your purse-strings quickly, or else I shall send you out of the land of the living.' Now the poor Quaker being frightened out of her wits at these bullying expressions of the wicked one, she gave him a purse of guineas, a gold watch, and diamond ring, and parted then as good friends as if they'd never fallen out at all.

Overtaking an old Grazier on Putney Heath, in a very ordinary attire, but yet very rich, he takes half a score guineas out of his pocket, gave them to the old man, and said, 'There are three or four persons behind us who looked very suspicious; therefore I desire the favour of you to put that gold into your pocket, for in case they are Highway-men, your indifferent apparel will make them believe you have no such charge about you. The old Grazier, looking upon his intentions to be honest, quoth he, 'I have fifty Guineas tied up in the fore-lappet of my shirt, and I'll put it to that, for security.' So, riding along both of them cheek by jowl for above half a mile, and the coast being still clear, the Golden Farmer said to the old man, 'I believe here's nobody will take the pains of robbing you or me today; therefore I think I had as good take the trouble upon me of robbing you myself, so, instead of delivering your purse, pray give me the lappet of your shirt.' The old Grazier was horridly startled at these words, and began to beseech him not to be so cruel in robbing a Poor Old Man. 'Prithee,' (quoth the Golden Farmer) 'don't tell me of cruelty, for who can be more cruel than men of your age, whose pride it is to teach their servants their duties with as much cruelty as some people teach their dogs to fetch and carry?' So, being obliged to cut off the lappet of the old man's shirt himself, for he would not, he rid away to seek out for another booty.

As the second story indicates, Davis practised his robberies at a safe distance from his home ground where he was too liable to be recognised: he seems, indeed, to have kept a house at Bagshot, near the main roads to the South and West from London, for convenience. It was in London that he was eventually captured, and executed on 20 December 1689, in Fleet Street, at the remarkable age of sixty four, after forty-two years of successful robbery. As a deterrent to others, his body was hung in chains outside his house on Bagshot Heath. A ballad published on the day of his execution, entitled *The Golden Farmer's Last Farewell,* puts most improbable sentiments of repentance into his mouth:

> I having run my Race
>   I now at last do see
> that in much shame and sad disgrace
>   my life will ended be.
> I took delight to rob
>   and rifle rich and poor,
> but now at last, my friend, Old Mob,
>   I ne'er shall see thee more.
> No tongue nor pen can tell
>   what sorrows I conceive;
> Your Golden Farmer's last farewell,
>   unto the world I leave.

Thomas Simpson

The 'Old Mobb' referred to in the Golden Farmer's Last Farewell is Thomas Simpson, and though there is no evidence that they were really friends, they were both pursuing the same business in the same part of the country at the same time, and it is most probable that their paths crossed in the course of their careers.

Simpson, who was born at Romsey in Hampshire not long before the Civil War, managed like Davis to maintain an outwardly respectable front to cloak his career on the highway, having children and even grandchildren to witness to his domestic qualities. Like

Thomas Simpson ('Old Mobb') stops the notorious Judge Jeffreys. (19th century engraving)

Davis, too, he seems to have conducted his transactions with the coolness that comes with maturity and experience. Thus, stopping a certain Sir Bartholomew Shower on the road between Honiton and Exeter, and finding he had little worth taking on him, he required him to draw a bill for £150 on a merchant in Exeter. Simpson left his victim tied to a tree in a neighbouring field, while he rode into town to collect the money. After some hours he returned and released his prisoner, saying, 'Sir, I am come with a habeas corpus to remove you out of your present captivity,' and, thanking him for the money, left him to walk home.

In the course of his career Simpson came up against several celebrities of the day. From Gadbury, a notable astrologer of the day, he took nine pounds; from the notorious Judge Jeffreys, Lord Chief Justice and renowned for his ferocity, he took fifty-six guineas. One day, working far from home on the London to Newmarket road, a lucrative hunting-ground during the racing season, he stopped a carriage in which was Louise de la Kerouaille, Duchess of Portsmouth and one of King Charles II's most eminent mistresses. 'Do you know who I am, fellow?' she asked, to which Simpson replied that he very well knew the King's whore, and added, 'As it is my trade to rob one whore to supply another, I must presume to take what you have . . . You may now say, Madam, that a single Highwayman has exercised his authority where Charles the Second of England has often begged a Favour,' and proceeded to relieve her of £200 in gold, a gold watch, two diamond rings, and a necklace presented to her by her royal lover.

Simpson's most entertaining exploit must have been carried out fairly early on in his career:

One time, Old Mobb being at the Bath, and understanding that a certain Lord was to set out for London the next day on horseback, but with a great retinue, he put himself in Woman's Apparel, and overtaking His Lordship on the road, and having a tolerable good face, as being in his younger years, the Noble Peer was pleased to scrape acquaintance with this young damsel, as he supposed her. So after a great deal of chat together, His Lordship being amorously inclined, he was for fulfilling the Primary Command, Increase and Multiply. Therefore putting the Question to her, this Masculo-feminine Creature, pretending great modesty, said it became her sex never to permit dishonesty to come nearer than their ears, but at last, giving way to her Inamorato's courtship, she told His Lordship, that was there any place of privacy, she should be very proud of gratifying his request; but to expose herself before half a dozen attendants, she would not for the world. His Lordship being very joyful at her condescension, they had not rid above half a mile farther, before a wood presented itself to their sight, where ordering his servants to halt till he came to them, he and his dear Bit of a Groat rid into the wood with an intention of enjoyment in the folds of love. His Lordship, for an introduction to the fort of pleasure, was for taking up the petticoats, and found under them a pair of breeches. Quoth he, 'What a Plague's the meaning of your wearing Breeches, Madam?' 'Nothing (replied Old Mobb) but to put your money in.' So putting a pistol to His Lordship's breast, he said, 'If you make the least resistance, you're a dead man.' Then binding His Lordship both hand and foot, he searched his pockets, in which he found above a hundred Guineas and Pistoles, and also took from him a Gold Watch, a Gold Snuff-Box, two Diamond Rings, and a Silver-hilted Sword. 'Damn my Blood and Wounds,' His Lordship cried, 'If ever I trust myself alone with any thing like a woman again.'

When Simpson was eventually caught in Westminster, he was convicted on thirty-two indictments, and hanged at Tyburn on 30 May 1690. Not a single charge of murder was laid against him.

James Whitney

Whitney was one of the earliest recorded instances of a man taking to the Highwayman's life as a way of bettering himself socially. Born about 1660 at Stevenage, Hertfordshire, of 'mean parentage', Whitney was early apprenticed to a butcher. Even in this trade he displayed a disregard for the law; it was while trying to steal a calf that he had his famous encounter with a performing bear which someone had put where he had expected to find the calf, and came close to cutting short his career then and there!

Either he gave up butchering or butchering gave up him, for he is next heard of as the landlord of a small inn at Cheshunt. It was a favourite haunt of Highwaymen, and despite a tendency to drink the profits, Whitney prospered modestly by harbouring the robbers, until it was suggested to him that he would do better to take to the Road himself: besides, it was pointed out, a Highwayman was a Gentleman, while an Innkeeper was not.

According to the legend, his first victim was a wealthy churchman from whom he took 130 guineas, and his second a poor clergyman in threadbare clothes, to whom Whitney gave some of the money he had just taken from his first victim. But despite his affectations of gentlemanliness, he seems to have retained much of his old manners:

Whitney and one more of his Gang, meeting with one Esquire Long on Newmarket Heath, they rid up to him, and honest Mr Whitney's first salutation was, Damn me, you son of a Whore, Stand and deliver! at which his comrade seeming to be displeased, cried to Whitney, Why can't you rob a Gentleman civilly, but you must curse and call names, like I know not what?

Whitney had other lessons to learn, as he aspired to be both a Highwayman and a Gentleman:

Whitney and his gang, meeting a Gentleman on Bagshot Heath, they commanded him to stand, whereupon the Gentleman said, 'I was just going to say the same to you, Gentlemen'. 'Why (quoth Whitney) are you a Gentleman Thief?' He replied, 'Yes, Sir, but I have very bad luck today, for I have been riding up and down all this morning, and as yet have not lit on a prize.' Then Whitney and his comrades wishing the Gentleman good Luck, as supposing him to be one of their Profession, they parted; but at night happening into an inn, where they overheard this Gentleman tell

The True Effigies of James Whitney, the Notorious Highwayman.

another, how he had saved an Hundred Pounds from being took from him today, by a parcel of Highwaymen, in pretending to be one of their Robbing Society, they were very mad with themselves to think what a booty they had lost. Hearing the Gentleman, to whom the story was told, say he had a pretty considerable sum of money about him, therefore if he should be assaulted on the Road before he got home, he would use the like stratagem, they swore they would narrowly watch his waters. So next morning Whitney and his Gang being out first, they laid an ambuscade for this other Gentleman, who suddenly falling into it, Whitney commanded him to stand, on which he cried, 'I vow, Gentlemen, I was just going to say the same to you.' Quoth Whitney then, 'Are you a Gentleman Thief, Sir?' 'Yes,' replied the Gentleman. 'Why then (quoth Whitney), as it is an old saying, that Two of a Trade can never agree, I must make bold to take what you have, wherefore deliver what you have presently, or else I must be obliged to send a brace of balls through your head.' These scaring words putting the Gentleman into a Pannick Fear, he gave 120 guineas to Whitney, who then taking his leave of the robbed Person, he desired him to acquaint the other Gentleman, whenever he saw him, that 'I was going to say the same to you' would never save his bacon again, for he should know him from a Black Sheep another time.

Though no doubt as Jacobite in his political sympathies as most of his colleagues seem to have been, Whitney saw the accession of Dutch William III as a chance of escaping the consequences of his criminal career. At this time he was heading a gang of some twenty or thirty men, and he offered to place them in the King's service for the war against the French in Flanders, in return for an amnesty. Unfortunately, the offer was not accepted, and so Whitney continued as before. On the 23 August 1692 he had the effrontery to attack the Duke of Marlborough himself, fighting a pitched battle against a patrol of dragoons near Barnet. It was one of his last exploits: four months later he was captured, together with most of his gang.

Again he tried to buy his reprieve, this time by offering to supply information about Jacobite conspiracies against the new King, but his captors soon realised that their prisoner had nothing of importance to reveal, and Whitney was sentenced. While at Newgate, he commissioned a tailor to make him a fine suit in readiness for his execution, so that he would make a suitably gentlemanly appearance prior to his final disappearance, but the prison keeper refused to allow him to wear it in prison, suspecting that it was part of an escape plan. However, his last portrait shows him finely enough dressed, so perhaps in the end he was allowed to wear it when, on February 1st 1693, he was hanged at Porter's Block, Smithfield, after giving the crowd their money's worth in the form of an hour and a half of last-minute repentance. 'He seemed to die very penitent,' observed his biographer: no doubt 'Captain' Whitney

The True Effigies of James Whitney, the Notorious Highwayman, as he awaited execution. (Contemporary copper engraving)

Whitney attacks Mr. Hull, a money-lender, on Hounslow Heath, and ties him backwards on his horse after he had sworn he would see Whitney ride backwards up Holborn Hill to his execution. (Martin's *Annals of Crime*)

would rather have had it said of him that he died very gentlemanly.

Whitney and Nevison, Moll Cutpurse and Old Mobb—a picturesque assortment of rogues, with little but their chosen profession in common. They came from widely differing backgrounds, and widely differing circumstances led them to the Road, but once there in business, they found themselves members of a unique aristocracy. Here on the King's Highway, a man's origins counted for nothing: now his talent and skill and courage were all that mattered.

There had, as we have seen, been plenty of highway robbers before Hind and Stafford and the other 'Captains', but this new generation of Highwaymen had established a new tradition, and all who rode in their steps could not but be aware of it. They might not all aspire to rival the exploits of Nevison, or to be portrayed in ballad and play during their own lifetime like Hind or Mary Frith, or to enjoy the posthumous glory of Claude Duval; but simply to take to the Road was a declaration that they were ready to play for the highest stakes.

By the close of the 17th century, the mould was set: James Whitney can be seen as the first of a new generation of Highwaymen who joined the ranks in full knowledge of the tradition and, seeing it as a means of social advancement, were ready to play the part that was expected of them. Of course not all Highwaymen came into the trade in this spirit. There were degrees among them: some courted notoriety while others were more discreet. Not all had the native courtesy of a Captain Hind or the French polish of a Claude Duval; no doubt many of them were just plain thugs and bullies. But fame was there to sort them out. The thugs passed from Tyburn to oblivion; only those who had earned it, went on to glory. But once their candidature had been approved, Legend gave their histories a helpful working-over, adding a little here, glossing over a little there, magnifying their virtues—their courtesy, their courage, their generosity—and going easy on their shortcomings—the killings, the ruthlessness, the sheer anti-social criminality of what they did.

And so the next generation of Highwaymen, matching themselves with their predecessors of the Road, had to compete not with what those gentlemen had been in reality, but with what Legend had made them into. It was a tough challenge; perhaps few would have made it, but for one fortunate fact—people still needed heroes, and new heroes are always preferred to old. So Legend was waiting to help the newcomers too, in their turn, on the far side of Tyburn Tree.

4 'There swing my gentlemen'

The great comfort of having it said, There goes a proper handsome man, somewhat ameliorates the terrible thoughts of the meagre tyrant Death.

(*Memoirs of the right villainous Jack Hall, 1708*)

Unless alleviating circumstances were shown, the penalty for highway robbery was invariably death. Acceptable pleas for mercy were hard to come by; almost without exception, the English Highwaymen mentioned in these pages closed their careers with a public hanging in which they played the principal part. The *Gentleman's Magazine* for March 1731 mentions one of the few who got away: a certain Sir Simon Clark, who carried out a highway robbery near Winchester in what seems likely to have been a spirit of youthful bravado. Caught and charged, he gave:

. . . a most pathetic and moving speech, which had such an effect, that there was scarce a dry eye in the Court. The High Sheriff and grand Jury, considering the antiquity, worth and dignity of Sir Simon's ancestors, the services they had done their King and Country, together with the youth and melancholy circumstances of that unhappy gentleman, agreed to address His Majesty in their behalf; upon which a reprieve sine die, which implies for ever, was granted them.

The trial of a Highwayman was not for his career as a whole, of course, but for a specific crime, and had to be conducted in the county where that crime had been committed. So though a Highwayman might be caught in, say, London, he wasn't necessarily tried there, but taken to whichever provincial town seemed to have the firmest evidence against him. For this reason Reading, thanks to its proximity to Maidenhead Thicket and other favourite haunts of the Highwaymen, was responsible for the conviction and dispatch of a large share. Maidstone, close to the Dover Road, and York on the Great North Road were other cities where many Highwaymen ended their careers.

The Highwayman's last days were expected to supply an aesthetically satisfying climax to his career. It was now that he could, for the first and last time, enjoy one of the fruits of his choice of profession: public admiration. Hitherto he had had to enjoy his wine and women, if not discreetly, at least clandestinely; now at last he could bask in open recognition of his status. The knowledge that it was soon going to come to an abrupt end may have cast a shadow over his mind, but heightened the senses. Dr Johnson observed that when a man knew he was going to be hanged in a fortnight it concentrated his mind wonderfully, but perhaps he could have added that it also sharpened his desire to enjoy the pleasures of the world he was about to quit. Though some, such as James Maclean, heeded the admonitions of the Prison Chaplain and wallowed in repentance, most condemned Highwaymen were resolved to enjoy themselves to the last and to the full.

Few, if any, complained of their fate. They had played for high stakes; for a shorter or longer period they had enjoyed a winning streak and all that goes with success, and now they had lost. It was all part of the game, and bitterness was rare. Capture was regarded as inevitable, sooner or later: they had seen their fellows taken and hanged, and now their turn had duly come. Did any of them escape the consequences of their crimes? If they had, we would expect that they would have become Legends in their own, very special right—the man they couldn't catch, the elusive Captain, the one no prison could hold. The public would have gladly made a hero of such a man if he had existed. The fact that no such hero emerges from the pages of history, that every one of the 'big names' ended on the scaffold, suggests that in truth any Highwayman of any stature eventually paid the penalty.

How was the Highwayman caught? Sometimes by members of the public, sometimes by parish constables: the latter had the incentive of saving the parish the cost of reimbursing travellers who had suffered loss, both had the very substantial reward of £40 offered for every Highwayman who was taken. For such a reward, many—such as the Fletcher brothers who so nearly took the Golden

Farmer—were ready to turn thief-taker when the occasion presented itself.

But though the offer of reward did lead to many successful captures, it was a system open to abuse. An unscrupulous villain could play the game from both ends of the field: such a man was that most accomplished scoundrel, the model for the hypocritical Peachum in Gay's *The Beggar's Opera*, Jonathan Wild.

Wild was prudent enough never to work as a Highwayman, but his trade depended on Highwaymen. From about the year 1710, he built up a steady trade in London, selling stolen goods back to their owners, naturally keeping a sizeable commission for himself. The arrangement was that a robbery victim would inquire at Wild's office about his missing valuables; the 'inquiry' would cost him a fee of five shillings, irrespective of success. Then, if Wild could arrange to return the goods, the victim agreed to pay half their market price, and to ask no questions. Wild would then give half of what he had received to the robber, and so the profits of the robbery were shared.

Such a system required, of course, that Wild should have an army of informers throughout the underworld, keeping tabs on every criminal and every operation they carried out. The result was that he had unparalleled opportunities for blackmail. Knowing every criminal and every operation he carried out. The result was that he moment, if he chose, he could turn him in to the authorities and claim the £40 reward. Consequently, he added a criminal protection racket to his other means of livelihood and became the wealthiest as well as the most powerful man in the world of crime.

In 1718 the law intervened to the extent of proclaiming that anyone who withheld information about a crime would not be entitled to the reward. Wild countered this by ceasing to charge for 'inquiries'. He still had sufficient irons in the fire; for, it goes without saying, from reaping the proceeds of a robbery it was but a short step to instigating the robbery in the first place. His sources of information were just as active in noting potentially profitable enterprises as in keeping track of those who executed them.

Wild pursued his many-faceted career for fifteen years: eventually, in May 1725, the law caught up with him. He was charged with stealing £40 worth of lace, with receiving it from the thief he had employed for the job, and with selling the lace back to its owner without making any effort to catch the thief. It proved hard to show that Wild had actually instigated the theft, though he manifestly had, but the second charge stuck securely. At his trial Wild claimed that he had brought fifty-seven criminals to justice, and tried to show himself in the light of a conscientious public citizen, but his true motives were only too apparent. He was hanged

A satirical invitation to Jonathan Wild's execution. (Drawn by Hogarth)

William Spiggot pressed at Newgate, February 1720. (Newgate Calendar)

at Tyburn, where he had caused so many Highwaymen to be hanged.

Wild was universally execrated, and it is doubtful if visitors came to see him in his Newgate cell except to revile him and gloat over his fall. The condemned Highwayman, on the other hand, was generally a subject of popular interest: admirers brought gifts of food and wine, ladies offered other favours. Of the Highwayman John Everett, sentenced to death in 1729, the *Newgate Calendar* records:

The minister of Saint Sepulchre's Church exerted himself to convince the prisoner of the atrocious nature of his offences; but the number of people who visited him from motives of curiosity took off his attention from his more important duties.

It was customary for visitors to give a tip to the gaoler in order to see the prisoner. Valentine Carrick, ex-officer and noted gambler as well as highway robber, called out to the gaping sightseers from his Newgate cell:

Good folks, you pay for seeing me now, but if you had suspended your curiosity till I went to Tyburn, you might have seen me for nothing.

Sentencing was simple and straightforward in almost every Highwayman's case: death by hanging, in public, at the nearest scaffold and at the earliest convenient date. Captain Hind, as we have seen, was quartered as well, but that is because he was convicted of treason rather than highway robbery. William Spiggot was another exception. When he was caught in 1720 and charged with highway robbery, he refused to plead either guilty or not guilty to the charge unless the effects that were taken from him at his capture were returned. This was a technical point: if he pleaded and was found guilty, as he must have known he would be, then his property would be forfeit to the Crown, and his family would be left destitute. By refusing to plead, he hoped to leave them something to live on.

But the harsh laws of the time had provided against such a contingency, and it was ordered:

That the prisoner shall be sent to the prison from whence he came, and put into a mean room, stopped from the light, and shall there be laid on the bare ground, without any litter, straw, or other covering, and without any garment about him, except something to hide his privy members. He shall lie upon his back, his head shall be covered, and his feet shall be bare. One of his arms shall be drawn with a cord to one side of the room, and the other arm to the other side; and his legs shall be served in the like manner. Then there shall be laid upon his body as much iron or stone as he can bear, and more. And the first day after he shall have three morsels of barley bread, without any drink; and the second day he shall be allowed to drink as much as he can, at three times, of the water that is next the prison-door, except running water, without any bread; and this shall be his diet till he dies: and he against whom this judgment shall be given forfeits his goods to the king.

Spiggot stuck this treatment until the pressure reached 400 pounds, at which point he surrendered: he was promptly found guilty and hanged.

Executions were conducted in public until 1868, and always drew big crowds. There was some pretence that public hanging acted as a deterrent and that the spectacle had a moral effect, but it is evident that, if anything, it led to greater admiration for the criminal. John Fielding, the eminent magistrate whose work we shall be noticing in greater detail later, had no illusions about the effects of public hanging:

The day appointed by law for the thief's shame is the day of glory in his own opinion. His procession to Tyburn and his last moments there are all triumphant—attended with the compassion of the weak and tender-hearted, and with the applause, admiration and envy of all the bold and hardened. His behaviour in his present condition, not the crimes, how atrocious soever, which brought him to it, is the subject of contemplation. And if he hath sense enough to temper his boldness with any degree of decency, his death is spoken of by many with honour, by most with pity, and by all with approbation.

(*Inquiry into the causes of the late increase of robbers, 1751*)

A few, such as Whitney whom we have already met and Maclean whom we shall be meeting soon, succumbed to the moral persuasion of the prison chaplain and spent their last days in repentance. A few others lost their reason when the time came: John Ashton, condemned to be hanged outside Newgate for highway robbery in 1814, diverted the spectators by dancing on the platform and crying out, 'Look at me, I am Lord Wellington!' At 8.20 the platform fell, but:

Scarcely, however, had the sufferers dropped, before, to the awe and astonishment of every beholder, Ashton rebounded from the rope, and was instantaneously seen dancing near the Ordinary, and crying out very loudly, and apparently unhurt, What do ye think of me? Am I not Lord Wellington now? He then danced, clapped his hands, and huzzaed. At length the executioner was compelled to get upon the scaffold, and to push him forcibly from the place on which he stood.

(*New Newgate Calendar*)

But for most Highwaymen, execution day was a day of glory, and their journey from the prison to the scaffold a triumphal procession. Crowds lined the route, cheering. It was de rigueur, when passing an inn, to call for ale, and to promise to pay on the way back. Many heroes of the day took pains to go well-dressed to their deaths, and ladies would present special favourites with nosegays of flowers. At the place of excution they would find that copies of their last dying speech, yet to be delivered, were already being sold by the pedlars, along with broadsheets containing ballads telling their story with extravagant detail and ludicrous woodcuts depicting the scene which had yet to take place.

Country gibbets. (Martin's *Annals of Crime*)

View of HOUNSLOW HEATH, *with the* GIBETS *and Men hanging in Chains*

Dodd delin.t   Malpas sculp.

An execution at Debtor's Door, Newgate, in 1809. (*New Newgate Calendar*)

In the earliest days, a prisoner was hanged by being set on a horse, the noose placed round his neck, and the horse driven away with a smart stroke of the whip. By the close of the seventeenth century, however, the horse was harnessed to a cart on which the prisoner stood. A French observer, François Misson (1650–1722) described in his Memoirs what he had seen at Tyburn:

The executioner stops the cart under one of the cross beams of the gibbet, and fastens to that ill-favoured beam one end of the rope, while the other is wound round the wretch's neck. This done, he gives the horse a lash with his whip, away goes the cart, and there swing my gentlemen, kicking in the air. The hangman does not give himself the trouble to put them out of their pain, but some of their friends or relations do it for them. They pull the dying person by the legs, and beat his breast to despatch him as soon as possible.

The horrors of the spectacle, as well as the opportunities for heroism, were gradually diminished as time went on. In 1783 the place of execution for London prisoners was changed from Tyburn to the Old Bailey, thus eliminating the long procession along Holborn and Oxford Street. Dr Johnson, rather surprisingly, considered this reform to be a mistake:

A proposal to punish Highwaymen by setting them to work on road-mending, put forward in 1779 by the *Malefactors Register*.

66

Sir, executions are intended to draw spectators. If they do not draw spectators, they don't answer their purpose. The old method was most satisfactory to all parties; the public was gratified by a procession, the criminal was supported by it. Why is all this to be swept away?

A further improvement was made in 1788 when, instead of a moving cart, a platform incorporating a trapdoor was substituted. But the use of a noose knotted to give instant death did not come for some time after this, and death could still be a slow business. There were instances when the prisoner was still living after hanging for several minutes. A Highwayman named William Gordon, not otherwise of any particular distinction, nearly made history in 1733 by an ingenious experiment:

Mr Chovot, a surgeon, having by frequent experiments on dogs, discovered that opening the windpipe would prevent the fatal consequences of being hanged by the neck, communicated it to Gordon, who consented to the experiment being made on him. Accordingly, pretending to take his last leave of him, the surgeon secretly made an incision in his windpipe; and the effect thus produced on the malefactor was, that when he stopped his mouth, nostrils, and ears, air sufficient to prolong existence issued from the cavity. When he was executed, he was observed to retain life after the others suffering with him were dead. His body, after hanging three quarters of an hour, was cut down, and carried to a house in Edgware Road, where Chovot was in attendance, who immediately opened a vein, which bled freely, and soon after the culprit opened his mouth and groaned. He, however, died; but it was the opinion of those present at the experiment, that had he been cut down only five minutes sooner, life would have returned.

It was a brave attempt, requiring sufficient courage to absolve the prisoner from any accusation of cowardice. But most condemned Highwaymen had no choice but to submit with resignation, and for the most part they faced their punishment with fortitude and even bravado. Perhaps Dr Johnson was right, and the final procession supported them; others must have been sustained by their friends and companions, and a few by the comforting words of the priest; many, no doubt, took a few last drinks to numb their minds. But we may also suppose that most Highwaymen were fortified on their execution days by the tradition to which they had made themselves heirs. When they took up the Highwayman's 'trade, they had claimed the respect due to a gentleman; now that they had to settle the reckoning, they were ready to do so with a gentlemanly grace.

5 'The air of a lord'

Beneath the left Ear so fit for a Cord
(a Rope so charming a Zone is!)
the Youth in his Cart hath the Air of a Lord,
and we cry, There dies an Adonis!

(*Gay, The Beggar's Opera*)

It was all very well for a man to stand up, style himself a Highwayman, and thenceforth claim the respect and privileges due to a gentleman. Something more than his word was needed. The Highwayman's calling implied the possession of valour and skill and panache, and these could not be feigned. Their reality must be authenticated by success, visible and tangible.

So we need not be suprised that most Highwaymen were out-and-out exhibitionists. As with all who have a vocation to perform in public—toreadors and actors and racing motorists—modesty would have been quite inappropriate, for it would have implied lack of confidence, absence of 'presence'; and confidence and presence were important to the Highwayman as to any other public performer. True, there were a few Highwaymen whose private lives seemed to betray no hint of their criminal activities, but such men—men like Davis the Golden Farmer—were the exception, and we would certainly want to know much more about their lives before admitting that they managed without the adulation that their colleagues required. Did Davis really confide his secret to nobody throughout all those forty-two years? Isn't it more likely that somewhere he enjoyed, discreetly and prudently, his share of the same admiration that his more flamboyant colleagues enjoyed more blatantly?

But if, more commonly, the Highwayman was a braggart and a boaster, he demanded the deference of others not simply because he felt it to be his due, but because it was necessary to him. Their esteem provided the stimulus he needed for his work. For, no question of it, his work called for all his faculties, stretched to the limit. To ambush and rob an armed stagecoach on the public road at midnight, a man needed both a bold heart and a cool head, quick wits and steady nerves:

It was necessary to the success and even to the safety of the highwayman that he should be a bold and skilful rider, and that his manners and appearance should be such as suited the master of a fine horse. He therefore held an aristocratical position in the community of thieves, appeared at fashionable coffee houses and gaming houses, and betted with men of quality on the race ground. Sometimes, indeed, he was a man of good family and education. A romantic interest therefore attached, and perhaps still attaches, to the names of freebooters of this class. The vulgar eagerly drank in tales of their ferocity and audacity, of their occasional acts of generosity and good nature, of their amours, of their marvellous escapes, and of their manly bearing at the bar and in the cart.

(*Macaulay, The History of England*)

The life histories of the Highwaymen were published not only in catchpenny form at the scene of their executions, but in continual reprints of *Lives of the Highwaymen, The Newgate Calendar, The Malefactors' Register*, the *New Newgate Calendar* and so forth. Superficially they purported to be disapproving, pointing morals at every opportunity—the frontispiece of *The Malefactors' Register* shows a mother putting the volume into her son's hand as a deterrent against pursuing such a way of life, while a gibbet can be seen in the distance through the open window. *The Newgate Calendar* regularly treats its readers to such philosophising as this, from the life of Thomas Butler, Executed for Highway Robbery:

There are few highwaymen who have lived in such a style of elegance as Butler; and by this mode of proceeding he eluded justice for a considerable time, as he used to dress in black velvet, laced ruffles, and all the other apparatus of a gentleman. Yet justice at last found him out, and detected him while in the full career of his wickedness. Hence let those who are tempted to the commission of acts of illegality learn that the steps of justice, though they may be slow, are sure; that it is almost impossible for guilt to escape detection; and that vengeance is the more terrible the longer it is dreaded, and the longer it is delayed.

FRONTISPIECE.

A Mother presenting The Malefactor's Register *to her Son, and tenderly intreating him to regard the Instructions therein recorded.*

Justice *Wisdom* *Fortitude*

Dodd delin.   Goldar sculp.

The anxious Mother, with a Parent's Care,
Presents our Labours to her future Heir:
The Wise, the Brave, the Temperate, and the Just,
Who love their Neighbour, and in God who trust,
Safe through the Dang'rous paths of Life may Steer,
Nor dread those Evils we exhibit Here.

Frontispiece to *The Malefactors' Register,* 1779

Title-page of Smith's history 1714.

THE HISTORY

OF THE

LIVES

Of the most Noted

HIGHWAY-MEN,

FOOT-PADS,

HOUSE-BREAKERS,

Shop-lifts and Cheats,

Of both Sexes, in and about *London,*
and other Places of *Great-Britain,* for
above fifty Years last past.

Wherein their most secret and barbarous Murders,
unparallel'd Robberies, notorious Thefts, and
unheard of Cheats, are expos'd to the Publick.

By Capt. ALEXANDER SMITH.

In Two Volumes.

The THIRD EDITION Corrected.

LONDON:

Printed for *J. Morphew* near *Stationers-Hall,*
and *A. Dodd* without *Temple-Bar.* M DCC XIV.

71

But it is improbable that the lives of the Highwaymen were read only because of the virtuous morals they inculcated, or that those who thronged Newgate to gawk at the condemned prisoners came only to satisfy themselves that Right had Triumphed and Justice was about to be Done. Simple admiration for the Highwayman's skill played a part: this is De Quincey's verdict, written as the great age of the Highwaymen was drawing to its close:

The finest men in England, physically speaking, throughout the last century, the very noblest specimens of man, considered as an animal, were the mounted robbers who cultivated their profession of the great roads.

They had of necessity to be first-rate horsemen, in an age when any man had to have a fair degree of competence in the management of horses. When Colonel George Hanger visited the condemned Highwayman William Hawke at Newgate in 1774, he offered to purchase his horse. Hawke, believing or pretending to believe that Hanger wanted the horse for the same purpose as he had himself employed her, replied:

Sir, I am as much obliged to you for your proposal as for your visit. But the mare won't suit you, perhaps, if you want her for the Road. It is not every man that can get her up to a carriage.

With skill, he had to have stamina, for his job required him to be out in the open in all weathers, sitting in the saddle for long hours by day and night, sometimes passive, sometimes strenuously active, riding hard to chase his quarry, riding harder still to evade his pursuers. And together with these physical qualities he must have intelligence, resourcefulness, cunning. It was not enough to have the valour to stop and rob a coach or a traveller; he must know which quarry was worthy of his efforts, know when and where to expect it, plan when and where was best to attack it.

Different Highwaymen had different methods. We have seen how Francis Jackson and his colleagues used sometimes to wait around in likely spots for what might come their way by chance, but also haunted places where valuable tips might be picked up. A favourite method was to overtake a traveller, fall into conversation with him, endeavour to learn if he was carrying anything worth the taking, and ride with him till a suitable stretch of road favoured a robbery. A few went about the planning of their operations more scientifically: Anthony Drury, in 1726, struck up an acquaintance with Robert King, the driver of the Bicester wagon. King would tell Drury when he was to carry wealthy passengers, and the two would share the proceeds. Clearly, if the Bicester wagon was robbed too recurrently, suspicion might fall on the driver; in this case, however, the two schemers were betrayed by an informer hoping to collect the reward.

A predator's reputation is largely determined by the quality of the quarry he preys upon. If the Highwayman had confined his attentions to farmers returning from market and suchlike lowly travellers, he could never have commanded much respect. That is why, in legend at any rate, the Highwayman is archetypally portrayed as challenging the stagecoach.

Like the Highwayman himself, the stagecoaches were the subject of legend and romance. The earliest coach services, begun in the

John Everett and Richard Bird rob a stagecoach on Hounslow Heath in the 1720s. (*Newgate Calendar*)

1660s, were rudimentary—cumbersome vehicles lumbering along rough roads, slow, unwieldy and easily attacked. They were therefore not employed by the wealthier travellers, who preferred the speed and relative comfort of the saddle. As the roads improved, so did the coaches, and so, in consequence, did the quality of their passengers and the attraction of robbing them. By the middle of the 18th century there were regular coach services linking all the major towns of England. The average speed of a mail coach was six miles per hour, a normal stagecoach four or five, a wagon two. By the end of the century these speeds had doubled: a coach was as highly refined as a modern racing car, a superbly constructed device whose management called for skill and expertise. The coaches competed with one another in speed, appearance and regularity as they swept—in one enthusiast's phrase—'down the road in glory!'

Such coaches were fit quarry for the noblest predator. Even at what seem to us low speeds, they were not easily attacked. Though in legend the Highwayman is generally shown attacking by night, in practice this would seem to have been the exception. Though night gave him good cover, it also made him a suspicious character and he could expect his prey to be more alert and on the defensive. He himself could also be more easily surprised. So he preferred daylight attacks, where he could make best use of cover, preferably at a point in the road where the coach was forced to move slowly—hence the popularity of Gad's Hill, Shooter's Hill, Shotover Hill—and if possible, where a bend in the road would preoccupy the driver with the management of his team.

The open country had many advantages both for the robbery itself and for the subsequent escape. But while it meant that there was likely to be a delay before help could be summoned, it also meant that if by some mischance there were men on the spot ready to pursue the robber, he would have difficulty in reaching a place of refuge. For this reason many of the less venturesome Highwaymen preferred the outskirts of towns, and particularly of course those of London. It seems astonishing today to realise that there was open country in the 18th century between Westminster and Kensington. In October 1715 Lady Cowper wrote thankfully in her diary:

I was at Kensington, where I intended to stay as long as the camp was in Hyde Park, the roads being so secure by it, that we might come from London at any time in the night without danger.

In 1736 Lord Hervey wrote from Kensington:

The road between this place and London is grown so infamously bad that

74

we live here in the same solitude as we should do if cast on a rock in the middle of the ocean; and all the Londoners tell us there is between them and us a great impassable gulf of mud.

Such circumstances worked wholly to the Highwayman's advantage. In 1740 the Bristol Mail was robbed in Knightsbridge, and in 1752 the Devizes coach. In September 1750 Horace Walpole heard a Highwayman pursued down Piccadilly after attacking a postchaise, and he himself, as we shall see, was robbed by Captain Maclean very close to home.

Thomas Quin stops a carriage in Drury Lane, circa 1750. (Martin's *Annals of Crime*)

At first, little attempt was made to defend the coaches: the driver had a gun with powder and shot beneath his seat, and that was all. As the activities of the Highwaymen increased, guards were added, armed with sword and blunderbuss. But stories of the self-defence of public coaches are rare: it was more likely to be the private traveller in his own coach who dared to make a fight for it. The successful Highwayman had to be careful which travellers he attacked. But he had plenty to choose from: by the end of the 18th century, some 1400 public vehicles a day were leaving London, and as many arriving. A proportionate quantity of traffic was moving in and out of the provincial cities, and of course these figures do not include all the private vehicles which might often be the most remunerative.

The most favoured haunts of the Highwaymen were strategically

Thomas Lympus attacks the Bath and Bristol postboy near Reading, 21 February 1738. (*Newgate Calendar*)

placed on the main roads leading from London to all points of the compass. To the North-West, Finchley Common, and to the North-East, Epping Forest. To the West, Hounslow Common and Maidenhead Thicket. To the East, along the Dover Road to the continent, Blackheath, Shooter's Hill and Gad's Hill.

Of all the various types of prey, the most popular was the mails, for this was most likely to contain money which was so much more convenient than traceable jewelry and other valuables. Astonishingly enough, in the early decades of the Highwayman period, the mails went by solitary postboys who, though fast, were very vulnerable. The *Newgate Calendar* commented:

This species of public robbery (mail robbery) was formerly, though never pardoned after conviction, very common. It is now matter of surprise to reflect that such vast property as always has been remitted by post-letters should have been so insecurely guarded in its conveyance. A lad with the mail behind him often carried thousands of pounds, through lonely roads, in the dead hour of the night.

As always, the same publication is ready to sound a moral note:

Robbing the mail is a crime of so enormous a magnitude, that we are at a loss to find language in which to express our abhorrence of it. It is inconceivable what distress may be occasioned by the perpetration of an act of this nature. Tradesmen who expect remittances by the post may be ruined by their not arriving in time; and the bankruptcy of one may be the destruction of many. Hence it is possible that hundreds of honest manufacturers, and other dependents on shopkeepers, may suffer through the wickedness of one man, who is base enough to rob the mail.

The authors seem to be more concerned with the risks to property than with any possible danger to life. When we consider the fact that the penalty for either crime was death, and that a man can only die once, it is rather surprising that highway robbery was so rarely accompanied by killing. Probably most of the Highwaymen killed sooner or later in the course of their careers: his biographers considered it worthy of special mention to point out that Thomas Simpson never killed a man in his life. But on the whole the Highwaymen seem to have avoided carrying personal violence to the point of murder unless they felt compelled. Perhaps they thought it would hurt their image?

John Hawkins and James Simpson attack a postboy carrying the Bristol Mail with a countryman companion, 1722. (Martin's *Annals of Crime*)

Before we look at the histories of some of the more eminent of the 18th century Highwaymen, here are some episodes from the careers of three of their less well-remembered colleagues.

Jack Withers (executed 1703)

One time Jack Withers and two of his hopeful comrades, having been all night a raking in the country, as they were coming a foot over the fields by Marylebone, by four of the clock in a summer's morning, they observed a Gentleman walking all alone, making all the gestures imaginable of Passion, Discontent and Fury. They, not knowing who he was, supposed he might be in Despair for Love, or some other cause, and so in that condition might lay violent hands upon himself. Running as fast as they could, for fear he should do himself a Mischief, they found him by the side of a Pond. Jack Withers cryed out to his comrades, Make haste, by God, tis even as we thought; the poor Gentleman is just going to kill himself for Love. So one taking him by one arm, and another by the other, they said, O! pray, Sir, consider what you are going to do; what a sad thing will it be for you to drown yourself here! pray be advised, and have better thoughts with you! Quoth he, What a plague is all this for? I aren't going to Hang, Stab, nor Drown myself for love; I aren't in love; I'm a Player only getting my part. A Player (replied Withers) if we had thought that, you should even have drowned yourself, and been damned too, before we'd have took all this pains to follow your Arse up and down: but to make us amends for our trouble, we shall make bold to take what money you have. So, being in a bye place, they tied his hands and legs together, and took from him about Ten Shillings and a silver-hilted sword.

John Smith (executed 1704)

had the shortest career of crime enjoyed by any Highwayman. After trying as a sailor, he turned peruke maker, but found the rewards insufficient for his needs. So he suggested to a colleague in the wig trade that they try their hand at highway robbery. His friend agreed, so next Sunday they rode out to Paddington and successfully robbed a solitary horseman. Encouraged by this success, they stayed away from work the following day and held up three stage coaches in Epping Forest; on Wednesday they headed west to Hounslow Heath and stopped three more coaches and a hackney carriage into the bargain. On Thursday and Friday they seem to have attempted nothing, but on Saturday they took to the road again and held up three coaches in the neighbourhood of Saint Albans. Yet, according to their history, their net proceeds from so many robberies was only about twenty pounds. On the following Monday, attempting to stop a gentleman's carriage on Finchley Common, they were caught and taken to Newgate Prison. They were charged and sentenced at the Old Bailey, and executed on 20 December at Tyburn, less than nine weeks after they had embarked on their criminal careers, and after a total of eight days as professional Highwaymen. As the *Newgate Calendar* reflected:

It does not very frequently happen that criminals are cut off after so very short a career as this man; but those who abandon themselves to the making unlawful depredations on their neighbours may be morally certain that they have but a short time to live, and even that this short period shall be filled with care, anxiety and perturbation. What a dreadful life! and how easy to avoid it.

Ned Bonnet (executed 1713)

One time, meeting a young Cantebrigian, who had more Money than Wit, recreating himself abroad in a Calash, with a brisk jolly Courtezan, belonging to bawdy Barnwell, a little village within a mile of the University of Cambridge, well stuffed with such sort of cattle, who'll sell the foul disease to a Gentleman, at a very moderate price, he made up to these gallants, and commanding them to stand, he very civilly demanded their money; which they refusing, he took the sum of Six Pounds, or thereabouts, from them by violence, and because they gave him some trouble before they would part with what they had, he was resolved to put them to some shame. Presenting a couple of Pistols towards them, he swore they should suffer no less than present Death, if they did not strip themselves stark Naked; whereupon, to save their sweet lives, they obeyed his commands. Then tying their hands behind them, he bound their legs one to the other, and slashing the horse, away he run upon a full trot with these Adamites, home to his Inn in Cambridge. But as soon as they came into the Town, such a multitude of Men, Women and Children were hallooing, and hooting after them, that the like, to be sure, was never seen after the Lady Goditha, when she rid naked thro' the city of Coventry. But their Shame did not end here; for the young Gentleman being called to an account by the Vice-Chancellor, for this Scandal which he had brought on the Collegians, by his publickly keeping Company with Lewd Women, he was expelled the University; and the Strumpet sent to the House of Correction, to do further Penance by way of Mortification for the Flesh.

(Smith, Lives of the Highwaymen)

Richard Turpin

> I hope, my Lord, you'll pardon me,
>   I'm not the worst of men.
> I the Scripture have fulfilled
>   though a wicked life I've led,
> when the naked I beheld,
>   I've cloathed them and fed.
> Sometimes in a coat of winter's pride,
>   sometimes in a russet grey,
> the naked I've cloathed, the hungry fed,
>   and the rich I've sent empty away.

(Contemporary ballad, Turpin's Appeal to the Judge)

Judged by his posthumous reputation, Turpin was the luckiest Highwayman of them all—a striking reversal of the observation that

Turpin in his cave in
Epping Forest. (Caulfield's
Wonderful Characters)

the evil men do lives after them, while their good deeds are buried. Since he was hanged in 1739 at the age of thirty four, his life has been told over and over again in great detail—and most of these details are fictitious. Even the most celebrated exploit credited to him—the ride from Rochester to York on Black Bess, to establish an alibi—was, as we have seen, not his feat at all, but performed by Nevison half a century earlier.

The false attribution of such facts is matched by an equally delusive attribution of fineness of character. In dozens of plays and ballads he has been depicted as generous and considerate, courteous and chivalrous, whereas the known facts of his career show him to have been quite otherwise. The hero-makers have had to subtract at least as much as they added.

The definitive version of the Turpin legend owes most to Harrison Ainsworth's immensely popular novel *Rookwood*, published in 1834 with splendidly heroic illustrations by George Cruikshank. But the process of transforming the commonplace villain into a hero of romance had started long before. We have of course already noted the tendency to adulate the Highwayman as compared with other species of criminal, particularly after he had been caught, but none of Turpin's confederates was to enjoy anything approaching his posthumous reputation. Yet on the face of it, Turpin seems to be most intractable raw material for plastic surgery. Why was he chosen from so many possible applicants? The bare facts of his life give us no clue, and we have no more intimate description to help us. But it is evident that he possessed that elusive quality, charisma; even in his own lifetime, even in the early stages of his career, he had a flair for attracting attention, which served as the basis for his future glorification.

Turpin was a farmer's son, born at Thackstead in Essex in 1705: his baptism is recorded in the Parish Register. Later his father kept an inn, now named The Crown. Young Richard was apprenticed to a butcher in Whitechapel, then went into business for himself at Waltham Abbey. He married an innkeeper's daughter named Hester Palmer. To help business, he went into cattle stealing, was detected, and had to run away to a quiet corner of Essex where he was supported by money from his wife until he found means of earning a living for himself—robbing the smugglers on the East Anglia coast, sometimes pretending to be a Revenue Officer. Such double ingenuity was lost both on the smugglers and on the Customs Officers, and he was soon on the run again. This time he headed for Epping Forest, where he joined a gang of deer stealers, selling venison which was smuggled into London beneath wagon-loads of vegetables.

Turpin stops the York stage.
(Lithograph by W. Clark, c.
1840)

But the rewards of poaching were meagre, and the gang graduated to more lucrative practices. Known now as 'Gregory's Gang', they became notorious for their burglaries in the north-eastern outskirts of London. From this time dates the story of Turpin's holding the landlady of an inn—possibly the Bull on Shooter's Hill?—over her fire until she revealed the whereabouts of her savings, a favourite trick of the *chauffeurs* operating at this time on the French side of the channel. With a growing list of charges of robbery and rape to their debit, the members of the Gang found a reward of fifty to one hundred pounds on their heads: when three of them were caught and hanged, the others dispersed.

It was now that Turpin took to highway robbery. A contemporary newspaper reported that a traveller was held up on July 10, 1735, between Wandsworth and Barnes, 'by two highwaymen, supposed to be Turpin the Butcher and Rowden the Pewterer, the remaining two of Gregory's Gang'. A fortnight later, the *Grub Street Journal* ascribed to them another robbery in the same district, and on August 16 reported that the same pair had robbed several gentlemen and coaches on the Portsmouth Road, between Putney and Kingston Hill. On October 16 its readers were informed:

We hear that for about six weeks past, Blackheath has been so infested by two highwaymen (supposed to be Rowden and Turpin) that 'tis dangerous for travellers to pass. On Thursday Turpin and Rowden had the insolence to ride through the City at noonday, and in Watling Street they were known by two or three porters, who had not the courage to attack them; they were indifferently mounted, and went towards the bridge; so 'tis thought are gone on the Tonbridge Road.

With such press coverage of their doings, the foundations were already being laid for the legends that were to come. From now on Rowden drops out of the picture, leaving Turpin to hold the centre of the stage alone. But soon he had a memorable encounter on the Cambridge Road with Tom King, another Highwayman of some reputation. Turpin challenged him, whereupon King laughingly replied, 'What, dog eat dog? Come, come, brother Turpin, if you don't know me, I know you, and shall be glad of your company.'

The two of them decided to go into business in partnership. Their base of operations was a cave in Epping Forest, located between the King's Oak and the Loughton Road, which was roomy enough to conceal their horses as well as themselves. Turpin's loyal wife used to bring them food and supplies. When the authorities ultimately found the cave, it was seen to be tolerably dry and comfortable, stocked with food and wine. The presence of women's clothing showed that others of the comforts of home were not lacking. According to some reports, Turpin had been making use of this convenient hide-out for six years.

His cave was discovered, and he himself nearly taken, in May 1737:

A reward of a hundred pounds having been offered for apprehending him, one Thomas Morris, a servant of Mr Thompson, one of the keepers of Epping Forest, accompanied by a higgler (pedlar), set off in order to apprehend him. Turpin seeing them approach near his dwelling, Mr Thompson's man having a gun, he mistook them for poachers; on which he said there were no hares near that thicket. 'No,' said Morris, 'but I have found a Turpin;' and presenting his gun, required him to surrender. Hereupon Turpin spoke to him as in a friendly manner, and gradually retreated at the same time, till, having seized his own gun, he shot him dead on the spot, and the higgler ran off with the utmost precipitation.

This murder being represented to the secretary of state, the following proclamation was issued by government:
'It having been represented to the king that Richard Turpin did, on Wednesday, the 4th of May last, barbarously murder Thomas Morris, servant to Henry Thompson, one of the keepers of Epping Forest, and commit other notorious felonies and robberies near London, his majesty is pleased to promise his most gracious pardon to any of his accomplices, and a reward of two hundred pounds to any person or persons, that shall discover him, so that he may be apprehended and convicted. Turpin was born at Thackstead, in Essex, is about thirty, by trade a butcher, about five feet nine inches high, very much marked with the small-pox, his cheek-bones broad, his face thinner towards the bottom, his visage short, pretty upright, and broad about the shoulders.

(*Newgate Calendar*)

With such a price on his head and his whereabouts known,

Turpin accidently shoots King. (Martin's *Annals of Crime*)

Turpin had to go on the run again. He was nearly captured while meeting with his wife in an inn at Hertford, and came even closer to disaster at Epping when the landlord of the Green Man inn laid hold of Tom King on suspicion of having stolen a horse for which a reward was being offered. King cried out to Turpin, 'Dick, shoot him, or we are taken, by God!' Turpin fired but hit, not Bayes the landlord, but his own comrade. 'Dick, you have killed me!' King exclaimed. Turpin fled and escaped, but vowed vengeance to assuage his anguish at his tragic error. 'Damn that Dick Bayes, I'll be the death of him, for I have lost the best fellow I ever had in my life. I shot poor King in endeavouring to kill that dog.'

History does not record that Turpin ever avenged King's death, but he continued to be active for a while. A contemporary newspaper reported in May 1738 that 'Turpin, the renowned Butcher-Highwayman, committed a robbery almost every day this month'. But soon after this, he transferred the scene of his activities to Long Sutton in Lincolnshire, where he was nearly taken for stealing sheep and horses, and thence to Yorkshire where he presented himself as a gentleman horse dealer by the name of John Palmer (taking his wife's surname). Here, away from his home

The death of Black Bess
(Clark)

ground, his situation was more precarious, and early in 1739 he was arrested and charged with horse-stealing. From York prison he wrote a letter to his brother asking for help. By chance the letter was seen by his former schoolmaster, a man named Smith, who had taught him to write and was able to identify Palmer as Turpin. On 22 March 1739, 'John Palmer, alias Richard Turpin' was found guilty of horse-stealing and sentenced to death. His last weeks on earth were spent in entertaining the visitors who paid to see the celebrated prisoner, in ordering a new suit to be hanged in, and in arranging for mourners to attend his burial: in short, he resolved to go out in style. At the Knavesmire scaffold he bore himself bravely, chatted with the hangman until the crowd grew impatient, then mounted the ladder and threw himself off with a firm resolve.

Notorious in his lifetime, Turpin became a legend after his death. The process is not easy to chart, but it is clear that he was given his quite fictitious horse, the indomitable Black Bess, by some popular ballad-poet. Horace Smith in 1825 published a version which contained the lines sung by Sam Weller in *The Pickwick Papers*:

Bold Turpin upon Hounslow Heath
his black mare Bess bestrode,
when he saw a Bishop's coach-and-four
sweeping along the road.

In the same ballad Turpin is described as executing a mighty ride from London to Gloucester in order to fake an alibi: this piece of fiction, altered to Nevison's York, forms the most celebrated episode in Ainsworth's novel *Rookwood* which set the seal on Turpin's reputation for ever. Since then, he has remained the archetype of the English Highwayman, bold and resolute, handsome and dashing. Forgotten are the smallpox scars, forgotten the roasted landlady; what remains is Turpin the hero, Turpin on faithful Black Bess, Turpin leaping the turnpike-gate at Hornsey, Turpin sailing over a farm-cart in Edmonton High Street, Turpin riding the North Road to York and everlasting glory.

James Maclean

Though he was called 'the Gentleman Highwayman', and in his dress and equipage much affected the Gentleman, yet to a man acquainted with good breeding, and that can distinguish it from impudence and affectation, there was very little in his address or behaviour that could entitle him to the character.

James Maclean, the Ladies' Hero. (George Cruikshank in Caulfield, *Wonderful Characters*)

The Chaplain of Newgate Prison was not impressed overmuch by James Maclean when eventually that celebrated Highwayman came to reside there for a few weeks, but his judgment was not shared by the public as a whole, who thronged to see the condemned criminal in perhaps greater numbers than any other Highwayman before or since. Yet his career on the Road had been short enough—four years at most—and the portraits do not show him to be strikingly handsome.

Maclean was born in 1724 at Monaghan, Ireland, but of Scottish family. His father was a Presbyterian minister, and his brother Archibald followed in his steps and became chaplain to the English community at the Hague. James was intended for a merchant's career at Rotterdam, but his father died when he was eighteen. This left him with a modest inheritance, which he took to Dublin and managed to squander in less than a year. When he returned to Monaghan he met with only a cold welcome, so took the best job he could, which was as a footman. His patronising manner with the other servants and impudence to his master lost him that job soon enough; in his next post, as butler to a Colonel living near Cork, he was caught stealing and discharged.

Maclean and Plunkett stop
the Earl of Eglinton on
Hounslow Heath, 26 June
1750.

For the next few years Maclean lived the precarious existence of a
needy and seedy adventurer. He joined Lord Albemarle's Horse-
guards, hoping for opportunities as a soldier, but changed his mind
when he heard the regiment was ordered to Flanders to take
part in the War of the Austrian Succession. He planned a journey to
the West Indies where it was said that fortunes were to be made, and
some ladies gathered fifty pounds for his clothes and equipment. He
gambled it away and instead married, in 1745, the daughter of a
horse-dealer named Macglegno in what is now Oxford Street. With
his wife's dowry of £500 he purchased a chandler's shop in Welbeck
Street and seems to have lived the life of a respectable tradesman for
three years until his wife died in 1748. Presumably it had been she
who had brought the business what success it had, for Maclean was
soon forced to sell up. He resolved to use the proceeds—£85—to
trap a wealthy heiress. Together with an Irish apothecary named
Plunkett who posed as his footman, he visited Tunbridge Wells,
Vauxhall and other likely spots in search of prey.

These muddle-headed plans came to nothing, and ultimately he
and Plunkett resolved to take to the Road. Though Maclean showed
himself anything but courageous in their first venture, they got
sixty pounds from a grazier returning from Smithfield. He had never
obtained so much money with so little effort, and this encouraged

the pair to further efforts. On Shooter's Hill and Hounslow Heath, at Saint Albans and as far away as Chester, they carried out a series of robberies with increasing confidence. But their reputation, too, was increasing, so Maclean took refuge for a while with his brother at the Hague, who had no suspicion of James' new way of life.

When he hoped he had been forgotten in England, he returned to London and to his life on the Road. He had lodgings in Pall Mall, and lived a gentlemanly life; 'he was well known at the gaming-houses, and was not unfrequent in his visits to ladies of easy virtue,' his biographer tells us. He explained his fortune to the curious by referring to estates in Ireland which, he said, brought him in £700 a year.

In November 1749, between Kensington and London, he stopped a carriage which happened to contain Horace Walpole, the celebrated dilettante, who subsequently regaled his correspondents with gay accounts of the encounter, rich in wit but short on detail. There must have been some resistance on the part of the travellers, for shots were fired, a bullet passing just below Walpole's eye, grazing the skin and stunning him.

In June of the following year Maclean stopped the Salisbury stage on Turnham Green. Then, riding westward, he and his companion met the Earl of Eglinton in his post-chaise, with two mounted servants more than half a mile behind. Maclean rode up to the postboy and threatened him to stop with his pistol; he kept the postboy between himself and the Earl, so that the latter could not use his blunderbuss. Plunkett, meanwhile, rode up and disarmed the Earl.

It was their last success. When they tried to dispose of the property taken from the Salisbury coach, some items were recognised from the circulated descriptions. Though he protested his innocence, Maclean was arrested and charged. Many witness came to testify on his behalf—Lady Caroline Petersham declared: 'My Lords, I have had the Pleasure to know him well: he has often been about my House, and I never lost anything.' But the jury were unconvinced and found him guilty without even bothering to retire.

At Newgate, Maclean seems to have been deeply repentant. Though many visitors came to see him—three thousand, according to Horace Walpole, on the first Sunday after the trial, including a great many fashionable folk—Maclean showed no interest in them, and devoted much of his time to exhorting his fellow-prisoners to repent. When he went to Tyburn on the 3 October 1750, he studied his prayerbook all the way and did not glance at the admiring crowds.

Turpin and Maclean were exceptional only because they achieved

The execution of Maclean at Tyburn, 3 October 1750. (Martin's *Annals of Crime*)

The Highwayman in heroic posture—William Parsons Esquire. In fact Parsons was a rather pathetic figure who was as big a failure as a highwayman as in any other calling he tried to follow. (George Cruikshank, in Caulfield's *Wonderful Characters*)

celebrity in a trade which, throughout the 18th century, attracted no lack of enthusiastic aspirants. They are unrepresentative, in that they won a larger share of fame than their fellows, but in most other respects they were typical enough. Particularly they were typical in one very significant respect, in that their careers as Highwayman covered only a small part of their life-spans. Even when they spent the greater part of their lives as criminals only a relatively small proportion of that life was devoted to highway robbery. Turpin was also at various times a cattle thief, a poacher, a smuggler and a burglar, and it was as a horse-thief that he was hanged. Maclean's whole life was lived on the frontiers of dishonesty, perpetually scheming to make his fortune by some deceit or device; he turned to highway robbery only when less blatantly criminal forms of adventure failed him.

So we are faced with a paradox: here is a trade to which its members are proud to belong, yet which few are keen to enter in the first instance. The truth is, there was hardly such a thing as a professional Highwayman. A man took to the Road only when his other options were withdrawn. So it was with Turpin and Maclean: so it was with William Parsons and Paul Lewis, with Gill Smith and William Page, with Gerry Abershaw and all those others who made their momentary appearance on the public stage, then left it for the next performer after giving their final performance on the boards of Tyburn.

To take to the Road was for most men an act of despair. Though the rewards might be high, they were not certain, and the getting of them involved both discomfort and danger in extreme proportions. Why would a man choose to be a Highwayman who could see any acceptable alternative?

Well, for one thing, as we have seen, there was the glamour. Turpin must have been pleased to read his name in the newspapers—if he *could* read—and gratified to see such generous rewards being offered by King George for his capture. But the knowledge that those rewards would inspire half the countryside to take him, must have made him reflect that here was a compliment he could have done without. Perhaps, for all his penitence, Maclean was not unflattered to be visited by so many and such distinguished admirers at Newgate; yet he must have wished he could exchange his present celebrity for that former obscurity which at the time had so sorely rankled with him.

Of course, even apart from the potential rewards and the glamour, the Highwayman's trade had a more direct appeal. It called for no special aptitude or skill, required no specialised training or prolonged apprenticeship. On his very first outing, a man might pull off a coup that a veteran would envy. Boldness was the first requisite—and despair breeds boldness. But to stay in business, other qualities were needed: a cool head, the ability to plan for tomorrow, the intelligence to know when discretion will pay off better than valour.

But most new recruits to the trade were not planning for a long career: it was only today's needs that concerned them. If they gave it any thought at all, they probably believed—or pretended to believe—that the Road was only a temporary expedient: a few quick successes to get them on their feet again, and then they'd return to a safer, surer mode of existence. In a few cases, they were able to give up the life—but only for a while. Sooner or later the need would come on them again, and they would once again chance their luck on the Road. The same incentives that lured them back, prevented others from ever leaving off. The rewards of a single night's work could win them more than they could hope to win by any other means; the next coach round the bend could bring them a week's, a month's, even a year's earnings.

If they had—as most Highwaymen had—a taste for wine, women and the gaming table, the fruits of their night's work soon vanished. If they did not have such tastes in the first place, they soon acquired them; for, mixing with others in the same line of business, they quickly learnt what mode of life was expected of them. The girls expected the money and the wine to flow freely; innkeepers expected to be rewarded handsomely for their protection; everyone looked to the Highwayman to put on a show, do the handsome thing, play the rake, gamble high, spend freely. And so, next morning, they must leave their doxies still snoring between the sheets, leave the rooms strewn with playing cards and emptied wine bottles, and take to the road again for more of the wherewithal . . .

Perhaps little or none of this could be foreseen and, even if it could, it was probably not so much these specific thoughts that deterred so many from choosing the trade, but a deeper premonition that to take to the Road was a step from which one could not turn back. Even if he did manage to quit for a while, he would go back—once a Highwayman, a Highwayman always. And so a man needed to feel something of a Death Wish, not so much a defiance of premonition as a fatalistic resignation to whatever fate might choose to throw his way, before he took his decision, swung into the saddle, cocked his pistol and directed his horse towards Hounslow Heath.

If he did indeed feel such premonitions, they were well grounded. Even if he managed to give the law a good run for its money, he was seldom far ahead of the constables and the thief-takers. He could prolong the process by switching the scene of his operations so that he did not get to be too well known in one place, but there were corresponding dangers when working on unfamiliar ground, with no trustworthy friends or safe places of refuge. He could lie low for a while after a successful venture, but sooner or later his purse must be refilled. And there were dangers in leaving the Road for a while: by the time he returned, his hand might have lost its cunning, his heart be less bold. Moreover, he might have lost touch with friendly innkeepers and other vital associates—and when every man's hand could be against him except those he regularly lined with silver, he needed all the friends he could buy.

No Highwayman ever wrote an authentic autobiography: those accounts which purport to give insight into the state of his mind are moral tracts which carry no conviction. We can only speculate what it was that sent a man onto the Road in the first instance, and what kept him there thereafter. But the words that the ballad-makers of the day put into their heroes' mouths must have borne some relation to their feelings:

> What mirth at Jovial's house of call
>   o'er wine cups our deeds to tell!
> To forget one day we must pay for all,
>   and swing high to the distant bell.
> Remorse too late this despised Heart
>   why with dungeon fetters bode?
> With courage I've lived, so with life I'll part.
>   Then Hurrah! Hurrah! for the Road!

> ('*Paul Clifford*')

6 Riding into legend

It is not altogether fantastic to claim that the heyday of the English Highwaymen came to an end because writers are so poorly rewarded. Henry Fielding wrote some of the finest things in English literature, but they didn't bring him in enough to live on. So he was glad to be offered, as a thank-you for writing political pamphlets on behalf of the government, the post of London Magistrate at Bow Street, Covent Garden. What had hitherto been a disreputable sinecure, a reward for government lackeys prized for its unique opportunities for lucrative corruption and abuse, became under Henry Fielding's administration a responsible civic post. In the exercise of that function he, and after him his brother John, laid the foundation of modern police systems throughout the world.

When he took over his new post, Fielding found he had a large staff, but all either weak or corrupt, and many both. No incentive was given them to work unduly hard to maintain law and order in the streets of London, and insofar as they put themselves out at all, it was rather to catch than to prevent, for the simple reason that there was a reward for capturing a criminal, none for preventing him committing a crime.

Fielding saw at once that what was needed was a salaried force. In 1751 he persuaded the authorities to give him a budget of £400 a year, and with this he started the first true police force. The six specially trained and dependable parish constables who composed it soon became known, and respected, as 'Mr Fielding's Men'. They had a retainer salary from the government budget, and on top of this were paid at the rate of a guinea a day plus fourteen shillings expenses by victims who rented their services. If six men sounds an absurdly small number, it should be remembered that they were not the equivalent of today's police force but more its 'Flying Squad', hand-picked men assigned to specific cases, ready to dash in pursuit of a criminal, day or night, at fifteen minutes' notice.

The scheme was immediately successful: several Highwaymen were taken in the first two years before Henry Fielding died. His place was taken by his brother John who, though blind from birth, soon proved himself as capable as his brother had been, becoming a figure of legend and dread among the criminals of his day. Inspired by the success of Henry's first scheme, John drew up plans for a force of message-bearers who would bring word to his office the moment a crime was reported, whereupon Fielding's informers, strategically located throughout London's underworld, would be alerted for any hint or scrap of information. It will be seen that his methods involved working with the system as he found it, infiltrating and exploiting the complex criminal world of London which had not changed significantly since the days of Jonathan Wild. It is not surprising that John Fielding was accused of following in Wild's steps and encouraging criminals to commit crimes so that he could then benefit from the consequences, either taking the prisoner and earning the reward for his capture, or arresting him and releasing him for monetary consideration; and in either case, taking a share of the reward for the recovery of the property. It would have been easy enough to construct such a machine for making money, and perhaps those who appointed the magistrates expected no less, but the charges were shown to be unfounded, and Fielding continued to press for more effective measures.

In 1763 Sir John (he had been knighted for his services in 1761) persuaded the government to grant him a greatly increased budget of £4,000 a year. With this he was able to form the first civilian patrols. His Foot Patrols comprised sixty-eight men in thirteen teams, eight operating in the outskirts of London, five in the city itself. Each team was made up of about five men, of whom the Conductor was paid five shillings a night, his men half as much: the Conductor was armed with pistols and cutlass, his men with cutlasses only. His Horse Patrols were made up of ten men, paid four shillings a night plus expenses, whose function was specifically to pursue Highwaymen. Despite the smallness of the force, their skill combined with Sir John's intelligence system proved extremely effective: the figures for highway robbery declined rapidly—so rapidly, that the government in its stupidity decided the patrols were no longer required and curtailed Fielding's budget.

During the last decades of the 18th century, success lay sometimes with the Highwaymen, sometimes with the police. In the year 1782 poor old Horace Walpole still had reason to complain:

We see by the excess of highwaymen how far evils will go before any attempt is made to cure them . . . I have lived here about thirty years, and used to go everywhere round at all hours of the night without any precaution. I cannot now stir a mile from my own house after sunset without one or two servants with blunderbusses.

(Letter to the Earl of Strafford)

Conditions did not improve permanently until 1805, when Sir Richard Ford obtained a government budget of £8,000, which enabled him to institute the regular Bow Street Patrols, on a scale sufficient to provide a measure of security throughout London and its surroundings. But other factors, too, were working to discourage the Highwayman. In 1797, due to the war with France and the resulting monetary crisis, William Pitt limited cash payments: this had the very practical consequence that far less gold and silver travelled the country. Instead the Highwayman's takings were liable to be notes or bonds, dangerously easy for the authorities to trace and so not nearly so negotiable. A stolen gold sovereign was worth a sovereign; a pound note was worth only the few shillings that a fence would risk on it.

The roads were improved, too, which meant that traffic moved faster, more people travelled by coach, and the solitary horseman, so vulnerable to attack, was rarer now. More effort was needed, with less hope of reward. And even the terrain in which the Highwayman operated was less favourable, as towns extended their borders and commons were enclosed. Sydney Smith used this circumstance satirically in a political speech at Taunton in 1832:

When I was a young man, the place in England I remember as most notorious for highwaymen and their exploits was Finchley Common, near the metropolis; but Finchley Common, gentlemen, in the progress of improvement, came to be enclosed, and the highwaymen lost by these means the opportunity of exercising their gallant vocation. I remember a friend of mine proposed to draw up for them a petition to the House of Commons for compensation, which ran in this manner: 'We, your loyal highwaymen of Finchley Common and its neighbourhood, having, at a great expense, laid in a stock of blunderbusses, pistols and other instruments for plundering the public, and finding ourselves impeded in the exercise of our calling by the said enclosure of the said Common of Finchley, humbly petition your Honourable House will be pleased to assign to us such compensation as your Honourable House in its wisdom and justice may think fit.'

Just how large a part each of these factors played in discouraging the Highwayman can only be guessed: no doubt it was the cumulation of so many obstacles on top of the reluctance we have already noted. But one factor seems never to have been a serious deterrent—the virtual certainty of the death sentence in the event of capture.

Historians of the period are fond of pointing out the enormous number of offences—223 in all—for which a death sentence was prescribed. What is less frequently mentioned is how seldom that sentence was in fact executed. Thus, between 1819 and 1825, though 7,770 offenders were sentenced to death, only 579 were actually executed. Juries and judges were not inclined to severity: since the death penalty was prescribed only for thefts of goods valued at forty shillings and more, they found remarkably often that property seemingly of considerable value was worth only thirty-nine shillings. The sentence then was only transportation: no light penalty, it's true, but not so very much worse than living conditions in the reeking courts and tenements of the London slums the wrongdoers were leaving behind.

But for highway robbery there was no commutation of punishment. The man who elected for the Road did so knowing that if caught—*when* caught—hanging would inevitably follow.

Once again we come up against the question, what made the Highwayman do it? We have balanced his potential rewards against his very real discomforts and dangers, the kudos attaching to his way of life against the very strong probability of his death. We have seen how his difficulties increased with better roads, faster coaches, fewer travellers on horseback, more restricted cover for his ambushes, stronger police patrols, the restriction of cash payments. And yet the Highwayman's trade continued to attract fresh recruits. Desperation? Bravado? Or is there some additional factor we have so far overlooked?

No theatrical performance for these many years has met with so much applause.

So, in 1728, the *Daily Journal* reported on the theatrical success of the year, Gay's *The Beggar's Opera*. It was a landmark in literary and musical history; it was the political scandal of its day, and it carried a social message so forceful that after 250 years it still has a remarkable impact in its own right, as well as when up-dated into *The Threepenny Opera*.

On the surface, the opera tells of a scoundrel named Peachum (based on Jonathan Wild) who manipulates London's criminals as

Gay's *The Beggar's Opera*. A benefit ticket for Mr. Walker the actor, by William Hogarth.

though they were his puppets. One of them is the gallant Highwayman Captain Macheath, who is in love with, and loved by, Peachum's daughter Polly. Peachum, for whom his robbers are mere convenient agents to be thrown away when they have served their purpose, has no wish to see his family connected with such a man, so he arranges for Macheath to be captured by the law. However, counter-intrigues secure Macheath's release and lead to the discomfiture of Peachum and a happy-ever-after finale for the Highwayman and his bride. The tone is sharply ironical throughout; the Beggar, who appears from time to time onstage as the author of the Opera, tells the impresario that he has planned for Macheath to be duly hanged:

Player: But, honest friend, I hope you don't intend that Macheath shall be really executed?
Beggar: Most certainly, sir. To make the piece perfect, I was for doing strict poetical justice. Macheath is to be hanged, and for the other personages of the drama, the audience must have supposed they were all either hanged or transported.

But the Player persuades him that this simply won't do, the public won't have it. So by a manifestly contrived switch of the plot ('In this kind of drama, 'tis no matter how absurdly things are brought about!') Macheath is reprieved and married to his Polly, with no thought of reform or repentance.

Beneath this surface satire, a stronger current runs, as the Beggar, speaking for Gay, points out:

Through the whole piece you may observe such a similitude of manners in high and low life, that it is difficult to determine whether the fine gentlemen imitate the Gentlemen of the Road, or the Gentlemen of the Road the fine gentlemen. Had the play remained as I at first intended, it would have carried a most excellent moral . . .

But of course the play's blatant lack of moral is the sharpest aspect of its satire. The reigning minister, the corrupt Walpole, had no illusions as to what target the play was aiming at, and though even he lacked the power to close the show down, he successfully prevented the performance of its sequel. But in fact, though Walpole not unnaturally felt that the cap was intended to fit himself, Gay's work has a broader theme, which explains its enduring popularity. Its more perceptive critics recognised this, when they blamed the opera for its unequivocal sympathy with its unpunished criminal hero. There is no question but that Captain Macheath the Highwayman is expected to win our favour, as against the Establishment as personified by Peachum. The Highwayman is represented as a popular hero, the lone-ranging Quixotic champion of the individual against the callous, all-powerful, all-devouring state.

Gay did not, of course, invent the Highwayman Hero. He found him ready-made in real life—a brief, violent, too-quickly-terminated life—and bestowed on him the enduring permanence of Art, where even if the hero pays his dues to society at the close of Act III, he will be revived by the time the curtain rises for the next performance. Gay's Macheath became an archetype, whose anti-social qualities could be overlooked because he was at the same time the representative of important social virtues—or at any rate of virtues which seemed important to the lower ranks of society. To them Macheath was one of themselves, Peachum represented the enemy.

For upholders of law and order—and especially for those whose job it was to enforce them—the model was a pernicious and a dangerous one. In 1773 Sir John Fielding felt called upon to ask David Garrick, the actor-manager, to suspend his productions of *The Beggar's Opera,* on the grounds that too many young men were being inspired by its apparent glorification of the criminal life to follow in Macheath's steps.

Jack Rann, alias Sixteen—
String Jack, sketched during
his last days at Newgate,
1774, by 'W.R.'

Jack Rann

No English Highwayman was ever more conscious of his role than
Jack Rann, who was born near Bath some time around the middle of
the 18th century. As a boy he worked first as a pedlar, then as a
household servant, then as stable lad and finally coachman: in this
last phase he developed his taste for flamboyant dress which earned
him his nickname of 'Sixteen-String Jack' in consequence of the
number of ribbons he wore at the knee of his breeches, a current
fashion.

He first came to public attention in April 1774, when he was
arrested with two confederates for highway robbery: the case failed
for lack of evidence, but in May he was taken again and charged
with taking a watch and money from a Mr Devall on the Hounslow
Road. He came into court with his fetter-irons trimmed with ribbons
and a nosegay in his hand. Once again, the charges against him had to
be dropped, this time on a technicality. Rann spent the evening
celebrating at Vauxhall, and paid for the evening by laying hands on
two watches and three purses.

In July he was up before the magistrates again, this time on a
burglary charge. However, Miss Doll Frampton, whose house he had
been caught entering, swore that what Jack was after was something
quite different, so the case was dropped. Sir John Fielding took the
occasion to warn Rann that his profession was well enough known to
the law, and that he had better tread carefully in future.

Of course he did no such thing. Several anecdotes testify to the
way he vaunted his trade. One Sunday evening in 1774 he went in
his finest clothes to the pleasure gardens at Bagnigge Wells, where he
boasted of being a Highwayman. In the course of a scuffle he
happened to lose a ring which he swore was worth a hundred
guineas—but no matter, he added carelessly, a night's work would
restore the loss. Eventually he became so insufferable that he was
thrown out of a window by the rest of the company, together with
his girlfriend Ellen. His bitterest complaint was less that he should
have received such treatment than that his friends should have had
so little respect for a *gentleman*.

In the same spirit he admonished a pair of sheriff's officers who
came after him for some little matter of a debt; while not disputing
their claim, he objected to the vulgar violence with which they went
about their commission. 'You have not treated me like a *gentleman*.
When Sir John Fielding's people come after me, they only hold up a
finger, beckon, and I follow like a lamb. There's your proper
civility!'

He seems to have always been aware of the law breathing down

Jack Rann on trial. (*Newgate Calendar*)

his neck, for there is an account of how one night he asked a turnpike-keeper, while riding through, if anyone wanted him. The keeper, perhaps a little surprised, said no. Then Rann said, 'I am Sixteen-String Jack, the famous Highwayman. Have any of Sir John Fielding's people been this way?'

'Yes, some of them are but just gone through.'

'If you see them again, tell them I am gone towards London.'

One might suspect a touch of megalomania, were it not that he really did command a considerable share of public admiration. When he appeared at Barnet Races, wearing a blue satin waistcoat trimmed with silver, it is reported that hundreds followed him, just for the sight of so celebrated a man.

In September 1774 Rann was arrested once again, for the robbery, in company of a certain William Collier, of Dr William Bell, a royal chaplain, on the Uxbridge Road. On this occasion there was at last concrete evidence against him, in the form of a stolen watch from the robbery, traced to him through a girlfriend named Ellen Roche. At his trial he wore a newly-ordered suit of pea green, a hat with silver strings, a ruffled shirt—and an unruffled countenance. Though he had expected to be acquitted once again, he heard his sentence with the bravado he knew was expected of him. In Newgate he kept up a brave front, throwing a party one Sunday for seven girls and himself. On November 30th the crowd had their last chance to admire his taste in clothes as he travelled to Tyburn. His career had

The Highwayman lives on.
Matheson Lang in the film
The King's Highway (1972).

been short and undistinguished in itself, but he played his part with a distinctive panache that earned him not only popular adulation but even a tribute from Dr Johnson: 'Yes, sir, Sixteen-String Jack towered above the common mark.'

And there, perhaps, we have a glimpse of that elusive additional factor which lured men onto the Road. For it is evident from the career of Sixteen-String Jack that it was not so much what a Highwayman *did*, as what he *was*, that told with the public. The careers of the later Highwaymen—of Robert Snooks of Hungerford, executed in 1802 for a single attack on a postboy, or of John Beatson of Edinburgh, executed in the same year for a single attack on a mailcart at East Grinstead—have none of the panache of their predecessors (and in any case who could make a hero of a man named Snooks?)

Such men were perhaps no lesser men than their forerunners, but whether because their opportunities were fewer or the obstacles greater, they failed to catch the popular imagination. Or was it that public attitudes were themselves changing, that the here-and-now reporting of criminal occurrences prosaically detailed in the newspapers could not stir the mind as the old stories had done? Nor, by any stretch of the imagination, could such people be seen as representatives of anything wider than their own self-interest. So the public looked back beyond Snooks and Beatson and Rann, back to a past already half transmuted into Legend. From a trait here, an anecdote there, they fashioned their own idealised version of the Highwayman.

Much of the credit must go to Harrison Ainsworth, who for the hero of his novel *Rookwood* took that ignoble fellow Turpin, erased his more squalid defects and bestowed upon him a constellation of better qualities which his original never possessed, and threw in for good measure exploits belonging to other men, most notably that dramatic ride to York that, if it belongs to anyone, belongs to Swift Nicks Nevison half a century earlier. Once Ainsworth had shown the way, many followed, until yellowback romances of highwaymen appeared on every station bookstall, and no Christmas Number of an illustrated magazine was complete without a stirring tale of the Road where the Highwayman is always handsome, brave and courteous—and a bit of a rake, too, to add spice to the story. His victims are fat, foolish men (though generally endowed with pretty, blushing daughters or wards). The police are pompous asses and all the hero's escapades take place at night, when:

Victorian idealisation. 'Your humble servant!' by J. C. Dollman in *The Graphic* 1888.

The wind was a torrent of darkness among the gusty trees,
The moon was a ghostly galleon tossed upon cloudy seas,
The road was a ribbon of moonlight over the purple moor,
  And the highwayman came riding . . .

(Alfred Noyes, The Highwayman)

Sometimes he was a cavalier, in high boots and plumed hat; sometimes he wore 18th century dress, boots no less high but now with a gaily ribboned wig. Either way, he was as witty as he was handsome, as courteous as he was quick-witted, so that it is no surprise to discover that he only took to the Road because he had been wrongfully accused of another man's crime, or cunningly evicted from his rightful inheritance by the machinations of a scoundrelly lawyer probably named Jasper . . .

Well, it's an apotheosis of a sort, but it's also a sorry decline. That pasteboard Victorian hero just hasn't the guts of his original. But there's little can be done about it now: legend is stronger than reality. Then, and now, and perhaps for ever, the preferred image of the English Highwayman is bold Dick Turpin, mounted on faithful Black Bess, galloping down the North Road to York and fame and glory.

7 'Kings of the mountain'

He waits, alone or with confederates, at a suitable point along the road. He sees a likely-looking traveller approach, he steps forward, displays his weapons and indicates his readiness to use them to enforce his request, and commands the traveller to hand over whatever valuables he is carrying. Then he takes his booty and makes his escape. This is the basic pattern of highway robbery, the bread-and-butter routine of the highwayman's existence, whether he works in the mountains of Sicily or on Hounslow Heath, in Sherwood Forest or the Abilene Trail.

In real life, one highwayman is very much like another: the differences arise from the variations on the basic theme, and are seen most vividly when reality is transmuted into legend. Factual accounts of hold-ups and raids and kidnappings, of resistance, pursuit and capture or escape, run to patterns whose repetition would quickly grow tedious. A sampling of banditry, as practised at different periods and in different parts of the world, will show how true to type most highwaymen run, and what scope exists for individual variation.

If one had to select any bandit as an archetype, one of the names on the short list would be that of Juro Janosik, who was born in Slovakia in 1688, and grew up in a world which was socially still back in the Middle Ages, with a downtrodden peasantry wholly under the dominion of a feudal aristocracy and virtually unprotected by a corrupt system of law and order which was far more interested in preserving the latter than upholding the former. It was

Romantic Italian bandit in Romantic Italian setting, ruins and bambino and all. (From a painting by Hess, early 19th century)

102

a classic breeding-ground for outlaws, hardly differing in any way from the 14th century England of Robin Hood and his contemporaries. Janosik at first enlisted in the army, but an assignment of guard duty over some rebel prisoners convinced him that he was serving the oppressors of his own people. At the age of twenty three he quit the army and joined a band of outlaws; in a short while his skill and daring had made him its leader. For two years he and his comrades roamed the Carpathians, robbing and murdering wherever they went, terrorising the population into supporting them. After only two years, he was captured. His defence put up the plea that he was a victim of injustice, but this was not accepted and in 1713, at the age of twenty-five, Janosik was hanged.

On the face of it, a simple and squalid history. He was a robber and murderer of purely local importance, whose career had been mercifully short and whose end suitably ignominious. Yet despite this, Janosik became a folk hero for the Slovakian people: literally hundreds of popular songs were composed celebrating his daring, his generosity, his love of his people and his country. Today he remains the most colourful and most widely known figure in Slovakian folk history.

In such cases, it is clearly local patriotism which imbues a commonplace career with a special significance. Spain had an equivalent in the Andalusian bandit Diego Corrientes (1757–1781) who like Janosik passed into legend after his career of banditry was cut short at the age of twenty-four. It was said of him that 'he robs the rich, helps the poor, and kills nobody'.

Such men are promoted to hero status by people living at the lowest social and economic levels, because they represent a challenge to the injustice of the world as it is. Men who dare not themselves defy the establishment can do so vicariously, if only symbolically, by honouring such outlaws. For the same kind of reason, though in a more complex form, they win the admiration of people in higher social levels who are no less aware of the shortcomings of social justice—particularly, of course, poets and writers. Schiller's play *Die Rauber,* first published in 1781, is the classic example. It tells of a young nobleman who, outraged by the injustice of society as he finds it, joins a band of robbers; he quickly becomes its leader, and though he disapproves of the atrocities committed by his followers, regards the pledges he made on joining them as sacred—there shall be honour among thieves if not in 'respectable' society. The machinations of the plot, which is the usual romantic farrago of good and wicked brothers, deceit and disguise, vows of fidelity and shattered dreams of happiness, don't concern us here: what is significant is the hero himself, the

A conference of bandits from Schiller's romantic drama, *Die Rauber.*

Jeremiah Grant on the
defensive. (Drawing by Phiz
for Benson's *Remarkable
Trials*)

university student whose social conscience forces him to choose the
outlaw rather than the establishment.

Schiller's robber hero is the upper class version of the folk hero,
and so comes, appropriately enough, from an upper class background. Here, fiction diverges totally from reality. Though so
frequently described as 'the aristocrat of crime' the highwayman
almost never comes from an aristocratic background, seldom indeed
from a respectable one. Robin Hood is sometimes made out to be the
dispossessed Earl of Huntingdon, but this is a very dubious detail,
not mentioned in most accounts, and very probably a spurious
addition added as a justification for his actions.

It is indeed one of the most attractive attributes of the
highwayman that he is a self-made man; that he raises himself, by his
own efforts, to equal terms with the representatives of the
establishment, the Sheriff of Nottingham or the local Chief of Police
or the Lord of the Manor as the case may be. He dictates, in effect, his
own terms, and by those terms he is as much an aristocrat as those

106

whose authority he challenges. Though the common people pay lip service to rulers who claim to be divinely anointed, this doesn't mean that they hold them in affection or esteem; they are generally delighted when one of their own kind sets himself up as their equal.

Jeremiah Grant, for instance, who was born towards the end of the 18th century, the son of a peasant in Queen's County, Ireland. The natural resentment of the Irish against the English dominion had been intensified by the French Revolution, and the resulting wars gave Irish patriots an opportunity for insurrection. As so often, it is not possible to determine where patriotism shaded off into criminality or vice versa, but, with whatever motivation, Ireland was beset by outlaw gangs, and any young man out of a job or in search of excitement was likely to gravitate into one of them. Jeremiah Grant was an outlaw before he reached the age of twenty, and by the time he was twenty-one he was his gang's leader.

Apart from the usual forms of highway robbery, the speciality of Grant's gang was levying an annual tax on local farmers as an insurance against robbery. As with any protection racket, its effectiveness depended on the ability of Grant to provide the protection he promised, and it seems that he was able to enforce this to such an extent that he was positively popular with his victims who preferred his single tax to indiscriminate banditry. We are told that 'at every farmer's table he was welcome, and the cottages that gave him shelter were sure of reward: for he freely shared the contributions he obtained with danger'. When he showed up at fairs and other local occasions he was treated as a celebrity, and—now styling himself 'Captain' Grant—was adored by the ladies: 'He danced with so much grace that the country girls were often heard to wish he had not been a robber'.

But a robber he was, and though 'his improvident liberality secured him the esteem and blessings of the lower orders', it is evident that his generosity was motivated to a large degree by the need to secure the sympathy and goodwill of the people among whom he lived. In course of time an informer brought about his capture, and crowds of visitors—including the customary sprinkling of 'fashionable ladies'—came to visit him in Maryborough Gaol. There was popular delight at the news that he had escaped, which changed to sorrow again when he was recaptured some time later, after shifting the scene of his operations to Wexford County and carrying them out under the name of Cooney. Again he formed escape plans, but on the evening planned for the break-out he was moved from Wexford back to Maryborough Gaol, where the evidence against him was stronger, and on August 29th 1816 he was executed on a charge of burglary.

'O la Borsa, o la Vita!' An Italian traveller gives up his purse to save his life. (Anonymous lithograph c. 1830)

The story of Jeremiah Grant raises one of the perenially intriguing questions with regard to the outlaw: the nature of his relationship with the people among whom he has to live, and on whom he depends for supplies and often shelter. Sometimes these necessities are yielded reluctantly, at gunpoint, or are obtained under an unspoken but only too apparent threat. Yet it is not at all rare to find that they are willingly given, and with them, sympathy and even support.

We don't know enough about the motivations of the sympathisers to establish positively what factors are at work, but we can certainly discount some of the commonly accepted explanations. The myth, in particular, that the outlaw robs the rich in order to give to the poor. Though probably a majority of outlaws do a certain amount of bribery, to purchase the goodwill of people whose cooperation they need, such gifts are more likely to be made to people with some power—law officers, important citizens—than to peasants whose goodwill is almost irrelevant to the outlaw's security. Sometimes a few judicious presents may be made as a public gesture, to win the sympathy of an entire community, but there is no record that any outlaw in history ever pursued a consistent policy of redistributing wealth on behalf of anyone other than himself and his band.

And yet the myth continues: people sincerely believe that the robber is concerned to help the 'little' people and attacks the wealthy in a spirit of social justice. How does it come about that people believed that Robin Hood 'did poor men much good' and that James Hind 'robbed the rich to feed the poor', that John Nevison is presented as claiming 'whatever I took from the rich I freely gave to the poor' and Turpin pleading 'the naked I've clothed, the hungry fed, and the rich I've sent empty away', that Janosik and Corrientes and Grant and so many others that we have yet to meet are all credited with a virtue they did not possess?

The answer lies in a parallel phenomenon which has been observed by present-day psychologists, studying the current outbreak of kidnap crimes, generally purporting to have a political motivation. A continually recurring factor, which complicates the efforts of those who have to cope with kidnappers and hijackers, is that their victims nearly always come to feel a positive affection for their captors, and sympathy for their motives, to the extent that they come to identify their own interests with those of the very people who are threatening to kill them, and actually resent the authorities who are trying to save them.

An early example of this is to be found in a case which occurred only three years after Jeremiah Grant was executed. One early morning in August 1819, an Italian surgeon named Eustachio Cherubini was summoned to an aristocratic home on a hillside near Tivoli, not far from Rome. On the way, he and the family's bailiff, who was conducting him to the house, were stopped by bandits who mistook him for the Prince, whom they had intended to kidnap for a ransom of 3000 crowns. Though they were disappointed to find they'd got the wrong man, they reckoned that they could obtain a ransom for him anyway; if none was forthcoming, they would simply kill him. A messenger was sent back to Cherubini's home town, with an order to sell the goods from his house and bring the ransom money: it was suggested that one of his ears be cut off as a sign that the kidnappers were in earnest, but the others agreed to save such gestures till later. Cherubini and his captors, with their other prisoners whom they picked up in the course of the day, spent the next two days continually on the move, sleeping in peasant huts or on the bare hillside, eating hard black bread and rainwater. At one moment the bailiff—who had perhaps deliberately led the surgeon into the ambush—quarrelled with the bandits; after a scuffle, he was thrown over the hillside to his death. A messenger returned from the town with a small fraction of the sum demanded, saying it was all that could be raised. He was sent back again with a message to Cherubini's townsfolk, that unless they received 800 crowns he would be murdered the next day. The surgeon had little hope that such a sum could be raised, and fully expected the night to be his last. Then one of the bandits came to him secretly, gave him some cheese, and whispered his assurance that the bandits would certainly not kill him:

At that moment, Cherubini recalled, I felt such comfort from the assurance of the outlaw, that he appeared to me to be an angel from heaven, and without thinking why I should not, I kissed his hand, and thanked him fervently for his unexpected kindness.

(Cherubini was ultimately released after the citizens of his home town had scraped together 600 crowns for his ransom.)

Is it legitimate to argue that what is true for the individual can be true for a community? Crowd psychology shows that groups are more easily swayed by emotion, less moved by logic; so I think we may risk a guess that Cherubini's emotional, illogical response to his captor for so apparently small a gesture of kindness provides a miniature model for the readiness of communities to feel a sincere gratitude to predators who have really done them nothing but harm. To earn such gratitude it is not even necessary for the outlaw to perform any specific act of kindness or generosity, it is enough, as in Cherubini's case, simply to refrain from carrying violence to the extreme. Any concession will be seen as a gift.

If this be so, it explains why so many outlaws have been supported, sheltered, fed and protected by the people they live among, even at real danger to themselves, and why sincere affection during the outlaw's lifetime will be followed by sincere regret at his capture and execution, a communal tragedy to be celebrated in requiem ballads and folk tales. It is doubtful whether any bandits have ever consciously recognised and played upon this tendency, for they, too, are unwittingly motivated by psychological forces which complement the attitude of the common people. They come to think of themselves as heroes and champions, holding their position by natural right and having a natural claim on the sympathy of their neighbours. Such a claim has no more logic to it than the others' acceptance: together, their complementary attitudes represent the twin halves of a psychological manifestation which can be traced back to the bid for authority made by the leader of a pack of wolves or a herd of deer, accepted willingly, and often with fawning gratitude, by those who are in no position to challenge it.

Highway robbery and kidnapping for ransom go naturally hand in hand. If a highwayman finds that his selected victim has little on him but has substantial resources or wealthy friends elsewhere, it is logical to do as the English Highwayman Thomas Simpson did with Sir Bartholomew Shower—tie him to a tree while riding into town with a signed order from the victim, as a condition of release. From this it is only a step to outright kidnapping for ransom. This has never been widely practised in England and is infrequent in North America—though recently it has become more common. But in continental Europe it has been a favourite device of robbers for centuries, and for 19th century travellers in the less frequented parts of Europe it was a permanent hazard.

An English clergyman named Rose was captured by Sicilian bandits about the middle of the 19th century, less than a mile from the railway station at Lecrera. A ransom of £5000 was demanded—an enormous sum for the period. When no money was immediately forthcoming, one of his ears was cut off and sent to his wife; when the money still was not paid, his second ear was sent, together with a threat to send him home piecemeal unless the money was paid. His wife appealed to the English government, who paid the ransom and then demanded compensation from the Italian government for failing to take proper action. A similar case occurred with Mr Moens, a British subject who was held by brigands from May to August 1865 until ransom money was finally paid.

Travellers in Spain were no more fortunate. In 1870, Mr Bonnells, touring near Gibraltar, was captured by bandits and ransomed for £27,000. Arthur Heseldin, captured in the Sierra Morena, was valued at £10,000, but was released for half this amount.

In 1870 a group of English tourists, including Lord & Lady Muncaster, were captured by the Takos band within twelve miles of Athens. A total of £50,000 was demanded. Negotiations shuttled this way and that, culminating in a bloody shoot-out during which the bandits murdered their four remaining prisoners. Takos and his gang were eventually either shot down by the military or captured and executed. Also in Greece, ten years later, a Colonel Synge, who was engaged in distributing food and clothing to Bulgarian refugees, was kidnapped from his farm by Niko, a well-known robber from Lamia, a Greek town on the Turkish border. Niko came from a family for whom brigandage was a hereditary occupation; there were twenty-five members of his gang when he seized Synge. A message was sent to the British Consul at Salonika, and protracted negotiations followed. At one point the British government sent two

Lord and Lady Muncaster captured by brigands outside Athens, 1870. (Griffiths, *Mysteries of Police and Crime*).

warships to the area as a show of strength but Niko was not to be intimidated by them nor by a force of five hundred troops sent by the Turkish government. The bandit insisted that he must be paid £10,000 and the ships must be withdrawn. The government gave way, the ransom was paid, and Synge was released after some five weeks' captivity.

On 27 July 1894, two French businessmen visiting Sardinia to buy timber were taken into the forests near Aritzo by a guide named Pirisi. Nothing was heard of them for four days, when M. Paty, the junior of the two men, reappeared and said that they had been kidnapped, and that he, not being wealthy, had been released to act as messenger to collect 500,000 francs in ransom for his companion,

Battle between the Sardinian police and the kidnappers of Regis Pral, August 1894. (*Le Petit Parisien*)

M. Regis Pral. The latter's father came over from Valence on the French mainland, and sent M. Paty with 10,000 francs, and this was accepted by the bandits. Pral told the authorities that he had been badly treated by the bandits, hit with a rifle butt and fed on barley cake. Inquiry revealed that the guide was involved in the plot and had deliberately led the two men into an ambush. Though Sardinia was wellnigh dominated by its bandits, the authorities had to take some action, and the police waged a series of battles against the bandits, culminating in a violent engagement a month after the kidnapping in which there were many casualties on both sides. A total of six hundred people were arrested for being members of the gang or giving them help.

In May 1891 the train from Constantinople was ambushed near Roustchouk in Bulgaria by a Greek gang of some thirty bandits, led by a notorious robber named Anastase. The hold-up was carried out in classic style, the line being ripped up and rails removed, causing the train to crash, whereupon the bandits attacked while the crew and passengers were still dazed. Five of the first class passengers, together with the engine driver, were held for ransom, and death was threatened unless the money was paid. A total of £8000 was delivered before the captive travellers were released.

In July 1895 the French journal *L'Illustration* reported:

Greek brigands rob a train at Roustchouk, Bulgaria 1891. (*Le Petit Journal*)

For years now, five or six bandit leaders, intrepid and audacious, have been spreading fear and terror in the Greek countryside. The government has done all it can to control the situation, but the brigands remained uncatchable, protected as they were by the same populations that they oppressed and held to ransom. The explanation was that they had their own special system of making themselves feared: they never operated in the district where they concealed themselves, but in adjoining districts. The accounts of their exploits came to the ears of those among whom they lived, with the result that they took good care not to offend their 'guests' in any way for fear of bringing a similar fate upon themselves.

The authorities found that there was in the end only one effective method of dealing with the bandits. Direct confrontation with sheer force was useless; nor was any help forthcoming from the terrified peasants who lived in the bandits' district. The only way was to stimulate an informer — perhaps even a member of the band who had his own reasons for wishing the leader ill — with a sufficiently large reward. By the date of the *L'Illustration* report already quoted, all but one of the brigands had been captured by such means.

The history of these Greek bandits tended to run to classical models. Thus Velios, in a situation so archetypal as to sound like the plot of a romantic opera, had taken a fancy to a girl in his town who didn't fancy him in return, not did her family approve. So he attacked her and cut off her hair; so her brother attacked him in return; so he killed the brother, whereupon he had no choice but to take to the mountains and become an outlaw. For a while he evaded the law, robbed and plundered with the confederates he had managed to attract and, in due course, was caught thanks to an informer.

The notorious Papakiritzopoulos began his career in similar fashion. Believing that he had been betrayed by his fiancee, he killed her and he too had to take to the hills and the outlaw's life. Though his conduct was that of the tradition-bound peasant, he was an educated and intelligent man, chivalrous in his behaviour and priding himself on being a gentleman. When an English aristocrat, travelling in the district, expressed a desire to meet him, the 27 year old bandit received him in style, welcomed him in English which he spoke as well as French, and offered him five o'clock tea and cigars. Evidently the two hit it off, for the Englishman remained as the bandit's guest for two days, and was then given a 'passport' to travel safely anywhere in the neighbourhood and to be given an hospitable welcome wherever he went. But such conduct didn't save him from the inevitable end. Tired of bandit life, and in hope of winning an amnesty, Papakiritzopoulos, hearing that assizes were to be held in his district, determined to kidnap the members of the justice

commission and use them to negotiate an exchange for his pardon. A messenger was sent to discuss terms, only to find that the local army commander, acting with unusual promptness, had already given orders for a military action. A bloody battle followed, in the course of which Papakiritzopoulos carried out his threat to murder the captured lawyers. By the time the fighting was over, every member of the gang had been killed.

Another gang, the Tsoulis gang, was betrayed in 1895 by a reformed brigand for a reward of 25,000 drachmas. In the same year a reward of 40,000 drachmas was offered for the Tsekouras gang, which inspired the local garrison to unwonted prodigies of valour. After coming up on the bandits as they were bathing in a mountain lake, the soldiers engaged them in a battle which raged for seventeen hours before the bandits were captured. To his captors, Tsekouras insisted that he was really a patriot, having killed many Turks and, when he was led to prison, he begged that he should not have his head covered with the customary mask so that the people waiting in the street could see 'the Kings of the Mountain'.

By the end of the 19th century, the last of the Greek brigands who

ARRESTATION DE NICOLAS JORDAN, A ANTEQUERA (Espagne).

Nicolas Jordan, the Spanish
outlaw, captured at
Antequera, 1884.
(*L'Illustration*)

NICOLAS JORDAN, BANDIT ESPAGNOL. — D'après les croquis de
M. J. Salles.

operated in Greece had been destroyed: the one remaining uncaptured was Tsanakas, who shrewdly committed all his crimes across the border on Turkish soil. In 1895 it was reported that he had already cost the Turkish government more than a million French francs in ransom money. But we need not imagine that no other robbers came to replace those who had been killed or captured. In Greece and in Spain, in Sicily and in Sardinia, they have been an enduring part of the social fabric for centuries and, as we shall see, in many parts they still survive into the second half of the twentieth century. Any social history with any pretensions to be comprehensive would have to take Janosik and Papakiritzopoulos, Athanase and Jeremiah Grant into account, as a social phenomenon if not as individuals.

All these robbers enjoyed local notoriety: some were recorded in history books, others merely in the ephemeral press of their day. Only a few achieved a greater fame as folk heroes, told in legend and sung in ballad. But they all have one thing in common. They were all, in a cultural sense, in harmony with the societies they sprang from. Bandits were part of the Sicilian or Bulgarian or Spanish or Sardinian landscape: that they should make their appearance in these places surprised nobody.

No less 'natural' is the appearance of similar robbers in newly settled countries, but here there is no historical continuity to ensure a measure of acceptance in the public mind. When the local police chiefs called out their men to do battle against Papakiritzopoulos or Tsekouras, one has the feeling that they were merely conducting the latest chapter in a history of conflict between the authorities and the bandits that had gone on from time immemorial, and that neither side expected the conflict to be concluded simply because an individual bandit chief was captured and executed. In these 'old' cultures, the confrontation between authority and the outlaw is an age-old feud, waged intermittently perhaps, but also unremittingly, so that a kind of ecological balance is built up wherein the predators are never actually exterminated but, at the same time, never allowed to extend their power beyond 'tolerable' limits.

In the new countries with their new cultures, no such historical background existed, and so here it was open warfare between the outlaw and the community. The extent to which banditry was able to establish itself depended on a combination of factors, geographical and sociological as well as political and historical; we shall find that these factors produced entirely different situations in the three most prominent of the 'new' countries—South Africa, Australia, and the western United States.

I

Southern Africa and Scotty Smith

Good bandit country must combine two nearly incompatible features: sufficient space to escape and hide in, together with a sufficient supply of plunder—which means settlements or travellers worth robbing. Southern Africa during the 19th century offered all the space a man could wish for, but had less to offer in the way of material inducement for the ambitious robber. The only period during which the booty became substantial was during the early days of the gold and diamond booms, and then the fact that the plunder was so rich in quantity, so concentrated in its source, and so important politically, meant that the would-be bandit was outclassed from the start.

Nevertheless, the Transvaal Gold Rush attracted its share of bandits along with all the other parasites that sudden wealth invariably breeds. Few of South Africa's robbers achieved more than local fame: Jack O'Reilly, Wilde Jacobs, Mick and Mays were all notorious enough in their own day, but have left little but their names behind. The only South African highwayman to have achieved anything approaching lasting fame was George St. Leger Gordon Lennox, better known as Scotty Smith, born in Perth, Scotland, in 1845 and claiming descent from one of Scotland's best known families. His claim has never, however, been validated.

Even Smith spent only a small part of his career as a highwayman. As far as the facts can be established, he left Scotland to fight in India—where there were always wars to be fought—came back and quarrelled with his father who wanted him to settle down as a farmer. He then went to Australia, where he killed a man in a quarrel and he may have become a bushranger for a time. Some accounts then take him to America, where again he had a quarrel, this time with a policeman, which forced him to be on the move again. Some involve him in the Franco-Prussian War of 1870, then with the unsuccessful Carlist party in Spain during the '70s. Finally he came to Africa in 1877, where he joined the army to take part in the Kaffir War, then found himself at a loose end.

At this point he started his legendary career as an African outlaw, beginning in the time-honoured fashion by stealing horses and cattle. Then he graduated by doing his first bank, supposedly to avenge a widow who had been defrauded by the bank. The second bank he robbed, so the legend has it, he did to help a friend who needed money to hospitalise his sick wife: having stolen the money, he told the friend to tell the bank his identity and 'find' the money, thus obtaining the reward. Meanwhile he himself escaped north to the Transvaal, where law and order were less prevalent than at the

Cape. Here he engaged in semi-political activity directed against the Boers, to the extent that there was soon a £500 reward on his head. These activities were diversified with diamond smuggling, horse stealing, cattle running—in short, anything that came to hand.

Compared with his Greek or Sicilian contemporaries, Scotty Smith is a shadowy adventurer, not a picturesque villain in operatic costume, but a commonplace rogue living on the edge of dishonesty with none of the bravura that leads a man to style himself 'King of the Mountain'. Yet legend did its best for him: besides adding Robin Hood motivations to his bank robberies, it tells how one day he rode up to a farm to find the widow who owned it in great distress. A £400 bond was due on her farm, and she had no money to pay it with. So Smith—somehow these robbers are always able to raise substantial sums of cash at a moment's notice—paid the widow's bond for her, then lay in wait for the landlord and took his money back again. Whether the story is true or not is beside the point; what is important is that legend attributes to Smith, as it did to Captain Hind two centuries earlier, a story with the Robin Hood touch.

Smith's busiest time was during the 1880s, when the traffic in gold and diamonds was abundant enough to provide the highwayman with rich rewards, but not so well-organised that the robber didn't stand a chance. Smith and others like him were able to rob the southbound stagecoaches with their precious stones and metals, then rob the northbound coaches with their provisions and supplies for the mining camps. Of the numerous raids carried out during this period on the routes between Kimberley and Pretoria, it is no longer possible to determine how many of those credited to Smith were in fact committed by him. What we do know is that their robberies were so frequent and so successful that soon the authorities had to provide protection in such force that the robbers were discouraged.

So Scotty Smith went back to his less lucrative but safer horses and cattle. Legend continued to favour him: isn't it a fact that once, while in Bloemfontein goal, he escaped for a few hours, pretended to be the President of the Orange Free State, appropriated the ceremonial coach, rode in state to the Parliament Buildings and, when it was all over, slipped back into gaol as discreetly as he had left it?

Yes, legend did what it could for Scotty Smith, but somehow things weren't quite right. Maybe he would have done better to stay in Australia.

8 'The Wild Colonial Boy'

He was scarcely 16 years of age when he left his father's home,
a convict to Australia, across the seas to roam.
They put him in the iron gang in the Government employ,
but ne'er an iron on earth could hold the Wild Colonial Boy.

And when they sentenced him to hang to end his wild career,
with a loud shout of defiance, bold Donahoe broke clear.
He robbed the wealthy silver tails, their stock he did destroy,
but no trooper in the land could catch the Wild Colonial Boy.

When English criminals of the 17th and 18th century were sentenced to transportation, it was to America they were sent. The Declaration of Independence in 1776 presented the judges with a problem; the discovery of Australia could not have occurred more conveniently. It was quickly recognised as a suitable dumping-ground for Britain's superfluous criminals, and the first convicts arrived in 1788. Those 'first-fleeters' may not have had quite so much cause for pride as the Pilgrim Fathers of 1620, yet they too formed a kind of faute-de-mieux aristocracy in the new colony. Before two years were out, one of them had laid the foundations of the bushranger tradition: an underfed prisoner named John 'Black' Caesar 'went bush', formed a gang and lived as an outlaw. He was twice caught and twice escaped; eventually he was shot in 1796 by a settler of Wimlow, after a reward of five gallons of rum had been offered for him dead or alive.

120

Tasmanian convicts plundering settlers' homesteads. (Drawing by Frank R. Mahony)

Many of the convicts had led a free-ranging life before being transported, and the lure of Australia's wide open spaces would have been a temptation even apart from the stimulus provided by the appalling conditions in the prisons and convict settlements. A steady trickle of escaping prisoners headed for the bush, there to live as best they could, preying on whatever came their way. It was a tough life — but convict life was even tougher. The situation grew sufficiently serious for the authorities to mount a sizeable campaign against them. With the help of mounted police, thirty-four bushrangers were caught and hanged in 1822, but many more managed to escape whether through skill or bribery. For nearly a hundred years, the natural hazards of living or travelling in the Australian bush were aggravated by the activities of men like 'Bold' Jack Donahoe, the original 'wild colonial boy'.

Like the majority of the Australian bushrangers, Donahoe was of Irish origin; he had been transported to Australia in 1824 at the age of 18, for robbery. After three years in the colony he took to the bush, and lived as his compatriot Jeremiah Grant was doing back in Ireland — attacking remote homesteads, rustling cattle and 'bailing up' travellers. He caught the popular imagination by his fondness for fine clothes, which he took from his victims along with their more valuable possessions. When he was finally killed in 1830, he was made the hero of the ballad we have quoted, which the authorities tried to suppress by threatening to withdraw the licence from any bar where it was sung. Such repression merely intensified the cult,

121

just as the efforts of the authorities to discourage bushrangers by the Bushranging Act, whereby suspects could be arrested without a warrant, had the effect of sharpening the determination of those who took to the bushranger's life.

Various names stand out. There was John Lynch (1813–1842) another Irishman and a religious fanatic, who sought God's guidance before he committed a crime—God generally told him to go right ahead. William Westwood (1820–1845), known as 'Jackey Jackey', who had been transported for forgery at the age of sixteen, was perhaps consciously imitating the Highwayman Duval when he forced his victims to dance a jig with him. Men such as these enjoyed a career of only a few years, sometimes measured only in months. It was a brief, desperate life of harsh and continual discomfort, relieved only by occasional bouts of drinking and whoring—and, while it lasted, the sense of freedom.

For a few, there was the additional reward of popular admiration. 'Gentleman Matt' Brady was a gentleman's valet from Manchester, who had been transported for forgery. In 1824 he escaped from a harsh prison is Tasmania (then known as Van Diemen's Land) and formed a gang to attack settlers and rob coaches. So successful were his activities that the police were forced to step up their operations to what amounted to an all-out war: in a single year they caught a hundred bushrangers, hanging them in batches of up to ten at a time. For two years, Brady eluded the law despite the introduction of black trackers from New South Wales. During this time he made a nonsense of law and order in the neighbourhood of Hobart, terrifying settlers and discouraging the sending of any valuables by road. Yet when he was eventually caught in 1826, the ladies of Hobart thronged the trial court and favoured him with flagrant signs of admiration, while to his cell they sent gifts of flowers, fruit and food. Nor was this hero-worship confined to the ladies: men derided the authorities as much for catching him as for having previously failed to catch him for two years.

> Frank Gardiner was a bushranger
> of terrible renown.
> He robbed the Forbes Gold Escort
> and eloped with Kitty Brown.

The discovery of Australian gold in 1851 provided wonderful new scope for the bushranger, and led to one of the most celebrated of the bushrangers' exploits: the attack on the gold escort at Eugowra on June 15th 1862. The leader of the attack was a bushranger named Frank Gardiner, who had been born in 1830. He commenced his

Attack on the Gold Escort en route for Melbourne, 20 July 1853.

122

career in the traditional manner as a horse thief but had been lead-ing a bushranging life since 1854, sometimes with colleagues and sometimes alone. For the gold raid he gathered seven others to form an ambush which so took the convoy by surprise that the police escort was forced to retreat. Gardiner and his confederates got away with gold dust and notes valued at £12,000, which were taken to their hideout and shared out meticulously on a pair of scales.

This exploit caught the popular imagination, and so did Gardiner's romantic attachment to a lady named Kitty Brown; it was while paying his mistress a visit that the bushranger was nearly captured by the police chief, Sir Frederick Pottinger, who, like all representatives of authority, was a figure of fun in Australian eyes:

> The joy of her heart is a bushranger smart
> who lion-like prowls in the night.
> With supper all spread—and a four-poster bed—
> she waits by the flickering light.
>
> Up started then Sir Fred and his men
> with cocked carbines in hand.
> They called aloud to the 'ranger proud
> on pain of death to stand.
>
> But the 'ranger proud just laughed aloud,
> and bounding rode away.
> While Sir Frederick Pott shut his eyes for a shot
> and missed—in his usual way.

> (Ballad, *The Bloody Field of Wheogo*)

After this scare, Gardiner made a try at going straight, but was recognised and arrested and, despite a popular feeling that because of his efforts to live an honest life he should be set free, he was sentenced to thirty-two years imprisonment. After ten years he was released on condition he left the country. This sparked off a political row which ended by bringing down the New South Wales government, but Gardiner was allowed to leave Australia and went to San Francisco where he ran a hotel until he was ultimately killed in a brawl.

One of Gardiner's gang was the celebrated Ben Hall (1837–1865) who, so the legend goes, never killed a man, never ill-treated a woman, and was always considerate to his victims. Even the reason for his taking to the bush was calculated to win popular sympathy: while in prison for a crime he had not committed, his wife eloped with a farmer. It was while in the desperate frame of mind brought about by this unkind act that he was approached by Gardiner and

invited to take part in the Eugowra hold-up. After that he continued
to ply the highwayman's trade successfully until in 1865 he was
betrayed for a reward by a former colleague, whose treachery is
commemorated in one of the best of the bushranger ballads:

> When the shadows broke and the dawn's white sword
> swung over the mountain wall,
> and a little wind blew over the ford,
> a sergeant sprang to his feet and roared,
> 'In the name of the Queen, Ben Hall!'
>
> Haggard, the outlaw leapt from his bed
> with his lean arms held on high.
> 'Fire!' and the word was scarcely said
> when the mountains rang to a rain of lead
> and the dawn went drifting by.
>
> They kept their word and they paid his pay
> where a clean man's hand would shrink,
> and that was the traitor's master day
> as he stood by the bar on his homeward way
> and called on the crowd to drink.
>
> He banned no creed and he barred no class
> and he called to his friends by name.

But the worst would shake his head and pass
and none would drink from the bloodstained glass
and the goblet red with shame.

(*Anonymous, The Death of Ben Hall*)

Of such stuff are legends made: Ben Hall has always been one of the best loved of the bushranger heroes, while his companion Johnny Gilbert, gunned down at the age of twenty-three for a reward, provided the model for the bushranger hero Jack Marsden in Rolf Boldrewood's classic novel, *Robbery under arms*.

Another man who passed into legend was Fred Ward (1836–1870) more generally known as Captain Thunderbolt. Originally from Windsor, England, he was transported to Australia and escaped in 1863 from the notorious Cockatoo Island Prison, Sydney. For six years he pursued a successful career—like Hall, never killing and never ill-treating women—and accompanied by a beautiful half-caste girl named Yellow Long who taught him his theme song, 'Her bright smile haunts me still', which forms a romantic part of his legend. He bailed up so many mailcoaches that the exceptionally high reward of £2000 was offered for his capture. It has been calculated that he must have taken more than £20,000 in his seven-year career, and with so little opportunity for spending it, a good deal must have been in his possession when in 1870 he was tracked down and killed by a trooper:

A moment's pause, a parley now;
the trooper made a push
to grapple at close quarters
with the 'ranger of the bush.
A shot, a blow, a struggle wild;
the outlaw with a shriek
relaxed his hold and sank beneath
the waters of the creek.
Twas thus the dreadful robber's
evil spirit passed away,
vanquished by brave young Walker,
now the hero of the day.

(*Anonymous, A day's ride*)

That ballad is one of the few which has any good to say of the officers of the law. In earlier verses the writer gives praise to both sides—'bold are the mounted robbers who on stolen horses ride, and bold the mounted troopers who patrol the Sydney side'—but in the end the bold Captain has become 'the dreadful robber' and it is the trooper who receives the hero's palm.

Ward's contemporary Daniel Morgan was an equally celebrated but less attractive figure. The son of a London prostitute and a costermonger, he named himself after the pirate Henry Morgan, and seems to have modelled much of his conduct after the same bloodthirsty gentleman. In addition to attacks on bush stations and travellers he made a speciality of payrolls, and by 1864 had a £1000 reward on his head. His brutal violence discouraged the informers on whom the police might otherwise have relied, and despite intense activity the authorities came nowhere near catching him. The police of Victoria openly jeered at the failure of their colleagues in New South Wales, and issued a challenge to Morgan who crossed the state line at the beginning of April 1865 and went on a three day rampage of robbery.

On the night of 8 April he bailed up a remote homestead at Peechelba and, taking his ease in the parlour, he insisted that the governess should perform 'Home Sweet Home' on the piano. A nursemaid said she could hear a child crying. Morgan refused to let her go and see what was wrong, but she insisted and hit him when he

127

Daniel Morgan shot down
by a farmhand, at Peechelba
9 April 1865 (Griffiths,
*Mysteries of Police and
Crime*)

tried to prevent her leaving. He laughed, said he admired her courage, and let her go. She managed to get a message to the police, who surrounded the house with forty troopers; with so many hostages, a direct attack on the house was out of the question, so they waited for morning. When Morgan stepped out of the door, unsuspecting, he was shot down by one of the station hands:

Shot like a dog in the bright early morning.
Shot without mercy who mercy had none.
Like a wild beast without challenge or warning,
soon his career of dark villainy's run.

(*Anonymous, Over the border*)

So great was Morgan's reputation that his body was put on show at Wangaratta, and respectable citizens posed for photographs standing beside the corpse with a gun in their hands. Locks of his hair were cut or even pulled out as souvenirs and a tobacco pouch was made from his beard. His severed head was sent to Professor Halford of Melbourne 'to advance the cause of science'—in what way, is not specified—but by the time the head got to him, it was no longer in a usable condition.

To judge by the price set on their heads—£1000 each, or £5000 for the whole gang—the Clarke Brothers, who were also active in the 1860s, were highly regarded in their day. But they have attracted less notice from posterity than Captain Moonlight who was one of the few Australian bushrangers with the ability to pass himself off as a gentleman. Intended originally for the Church, he periodically reverted to preaching in the course of a picturesque career which may even have included working as an engineer with Garibaldi's revolutionaries in Italy. So respectable was his appearance that when, after a bank robbery at Melbourne in 1869, a cashier swore that he could identify the voice of the masked robber as a regular client named Scott (the Captain's real name was Andrew George Scott) nobody believed him and the cashier was himself arrested on suspicion. However, Captain Moonlight thought it better to move on to Sydney, where he set himself up in society and flourished until an arrest for fraud. After serving an eighteen-month sentence he was released, but then arrested for the Melbourne bank robbery. He escaped, was recaptured, and sentenced for a further eight years.

He was a model prisoner, using his preaching abilities to lecture his fellow-convicts on the evils of crime, and even after his release he toured the country giving lectures on life in prison. But he failed to practise what he preached; before long he was working the bush again. In November 1879 a raid on a bush station led to a pitched battle with the police. After one of his gang, Gus Wernicke, had died uttering the pathetic words, 'Oh God, I'm shot and I'm only fifteen!' Scott surrendered and was hanged shortly after.

Unlike the English Highwaymen, most of whom ended on the scaffold, the Australian bushrangers mostly escaped execution. A good many, it's true, escaped it only by being shot down by their pursuers, but of those who were taken alive probably a majority were sentenced to imprisonment rather than death. This was the case with another celebrated bushranger of the 1860s, Harry Power, yet another Irish immigrant and yet another robber who commenced his career as a horse thief. After wounding a policeman he was arrested and sentenced to fourteen years; he served most of his term, then seized a sudden chance and escaped to Victoria where for a considerable time he worked as a highwayman. In May 1870 an informer led the police to his hiding place. He gave himself up without a fight and was sentenced to a further fourteen years. This time he served his full time, was released, and disappeared from history, leaving only a legend as one of Australia's best-liked bushranger heroes.

But Harry Power had one further contribution to bushranger history. For legend has it that among those who worked with Power

Harry Power and a fair victim. (Maurice Greiffenhagen in the *Sphere* 1900)

Capture of Harry Power by Superintendents Nicholson and Hare.

and learned from him the tricks of the highwayman's trade was that most celebrated of all Australian outlaws, a hero fit to rank with Robin Hood and Dick Turpin and Jesse James—Ned Kelly.

Ned Kelly

Ned Kelly presents one of the basic problems of the outlaw myth in particularly vivid form. His admirers claim that the Kelly family were persecuted by the authorities from the outset, and that Ned never had a chance—he had to take to robbery because the police

Kelly photographed the day before his execution.

left him no option. His detractors insist that the Kellys were notoriously regardless of law, unrepentant ne'er-do-wells ready to 'appropriate' anything that came their way, born to a tradition of take-your-chance opportunism which made the police their natural enemy. Both versions are probably more or less true. The Kelly family, like so many Australian immigrants, found that survival required them to live permanently on the edge of the law, a continual threat to authority. What aggravated matters was that, with the Australian's passionate belief in individual freedom, the Kellys enjoyed a popularity and prestige, regardless of what crimes they committed, simply on account of their uncompromising defiance of law and order. Conflict was inevitable.

131

Kelly's cave in the
Strathbogie ranges.

It was not long in coming to Ned Kelly. Born in 1855, he was only fourteen years old when a Chinese trader accused him of assaulting him with the words, 'I'm a bushranger, give up your money or I'll beat you to death!' and commencing then and there to beat the man up. Kelly was taken in charge, but the family claimed that the Chinaman had imagined the threat and presented a simple quarrel as a vicious attack. For lack of evidence, Kelly was released. But now the police had their eye on him, and had doubtless heard the rumour that he was working as junior partner to the well-known bushranger Harry Power, who was a tenant in one of Mrs Kelly's properties. Ned was reputed the best horseman in the district, a crack-shot and a good fighter. Over the next two years—while he was only sixteen or seventeen—he was three times arrested, though only once convicted. After serving six months for attacking a hawker, he was released—only to be arrested again three weeks later for stealing a horse. On the face of it, there seems little question but that Ned was being subjected to police harassment; equally it seems that they had good cause, for even his admirers do not dispute that he was engaged in stealing horses and cattle at this period.

In 1877 occurred the confused affair which set Ned Kelly off on his bushranging career. The facts are still very much in dispute, and from the conflicting versions one can only make a guess at what happened. The police seem to have visited the Kelly house in an outwardly friendly manner; drinks were served, and inevitably recriminations were exchanged. A quarrel broke out which led to Ned attacking a constable and hostilities escalated to a point where Ned's mother was arrested and he himself had to take flight. He was declared an outlaw and a reward offered for him dead or alive. He was any man's target, to be shot on sight and no questions asked, and £100 for his killer.

In the absence of any sure knowledge, it seems only fair to apportion the rights and wrongs of this affair in equal measure. The scene, after all, is not difficult to picture: the drinking, the exchange of accusations half-bantering at first, becoming more cutting as the whisky glasses are refilled. Some policeman goes too far, makes some observation too provocative to be accepted and Ned Kelly allows himself to be provoked—and so, in the time-honoured fashion, from words to blows . . . Without question, the police were being vindictive—equally without question, they had cause.

A police party pursued Kelly into the bush, but they had not yet taken the measure of the man they were after. Camped in Stringybark Creek, preparing to attack the outlaw and his friends, they were themselves ambushed: three were killed, the fourth got away wounded.

A Sergeant and three Constables
    set out from Mansfield Town,
near the end of last October
    for to hunt the Kellys down.
So they travelled to the Wombat
    and they thought it quite a lark
when they camped upon the borders
    of a creek called Stringybark . . .

. . . but brave Kelly muttered sadly
    as he loaded up his gun,
Oh, what a bloody pity
    that the bastard tried to run.

(*Ballad of the Wombat Range*)

Despite the killing, the Stringybark incident made Kelly a popular hero. In Melbourne's Princess Theatre a play entitled *The Vulture of the Wombat Ranges* had a bushranger hero patently modelled on Ned, and ballads in his praise circulated throughout the country:

Oh Paddy dear, and did you hear
    the news that's going round?
On the head of bold Ned Kelly
    they have placed two thousand pound.

And on Steve Hart, Joe Byrne and Dan
    two thousand more they'd give,
but if the price was doubled, boys,
    the Kelly Gang would live.

On 9 December 1878 the Kelly Gang robbed the Euroa National Bank of £2000 in a raid which, in Major Arthur Griffiths' words, 'rivals any criminal exploit on record . . . A masterly operation, conducted from first to last with cool judgement and the most determined strength of purpose. Ned Kelly, the captain of the gang, had planned the whole affair with all the foresight and precision of a general in the field; every detail was executed by his well-disciplined followers with the unhesitating exactitude of soldiers implicitly obeying the orders of their chief.'

On the previous day, the Kellys had stuck up a nearby homestead, made all its inhabitants prisoners—twenty-three in all. To these were added any others who came to the station till the Kellys were holding more than thirty people at gunpoint. With this operating base secure, the Kellys rode into the town, some three miles away, and set off for the bank. As they had planned, the bank was officially closed but the staff were still on the premises. One of Kelly's men persuaded them to open up and next moment the outlaws were inside with guns presented. The money and valuables were quickly gathered up, and the entire staff of the bank were packed into a hawker's van and a buggy from the homestead and taken to join the other prisoners at the base. They were warned not to make any attempt to move for three hours, with a threat to the station manager that if there was any such attempt he would be held personally responsible and shot dead. Then the outlaws saddled up and headed with their day's loot for their hiding place in the Strathbogie ranges.

The raid caught the imagination of the country, and further details made Ned more of a hero than ever. It was reported that the female prisoners at the Younghusband homestead had said 'Ned Kelly is a gentleman'. It was told how the money from the raid had been sent to the outlaws' families, with the promise 'There's plenty more where that came from. We have an account in every bank in Australia'. The authorities put the reward money up to £4000—in vain. When twenty known sympathisers with the Kellys were arrested and held without charge or trial, Ned wrote an open letter of protest to the authorities, enhancing his image yet further.

In February 1879—according to some accounts, because by now all the proceeds from Euroa had been given away or spent on debauchery—the Kelly Gang made another spectacular bank raid, this time on Jerilderie in New South Wales. The outlaws took over the entire township, including its four hotels, its telegraph office and its bank; even the police station was secured after the two-man force had been lured to one of the hotels to deal with a supposed killing. Besides the £2000 they got from the bank, Kelly's gang took many other valuables from the inhabitants and then, after hours of drinking and merrymaking—including riding drunkenly up and down the main street crying 'Hurrah for the good old days of Morgan and Ben Hall!'—they rode away. The authorities pushed the reward up to £8000, and the ballad-writers got busy again:

> It's when they robbed the Euroa Bank,
>   you said they'd be run down.
> But now they've robbed another,
>   that's in Jerilderie town.
> That's in Jerilderie town, my boys,
>   and we're here to take their part,
> and shout again, Long may they reign—
>   the Kellys, Byrne and Hart!

Now the police were more determined than ever, but they had to contend with a greater public sympathy for the outlaws than ever. The Kellys had friends everywhere, people who counted it a privilege to assist them. And if the rewards on their heads were high, the outlaws could match them with presents from their bank takings. The authorities did what they could to dent Kelly's image; thus the *Williamstown Advertiser* informed its readers that 'he spends his money among harlots in whose sweet society he is now basking'. But most of Kelly's sympathisers knew better: Ned might have had his pick of half the girls in Australia, but his way of life gave him few opportunities for social pleasures. The popular song might praise the life:

> If you want a spree,
>   come with me and you'll see
> how grand it is to be
>   in the bold Kelly Gang!

135

The attack on Glenrowan. (Drawing by W. Hatherell)

In truth it was a harsh, bitter life, where occasional outbursts of high living could not compensate for the perennial sense of danger, the discomfort, the loneliness.

In 1880 a curious report came to the notice of the police of a theft of cast iron. Shortly after, an informer claimed that Kelly was responsible for the theft and was using it to make armour for himself and his men. In June that year, another informer, a man named Sherritt, was killed by the gang. The police decided to make a large-scale attack on the elusive outlaw. News of the plan came to Kelly via his sympathisers, and he prepared a superb counter-plan. He would establish himself at a place named Glenrowan, to which the police would be coming by special train; he would derail the train and ambush its occupants. In the resulting chaos, he and his men would make their getaway and, with so many police occupied in the raid, they would make a series of bank raids in relative security.

The first stages of the plan went well. The small settlement of Glenrowan was taken over by the outlaws, all the inhabitants packed into the hotel. But then the first misfortune occurred, the engine of the special train developed a brake fault, which meant that another locomotive had to go ahead to clear the line. Meanwhile a

Glenrowan schoolteacher managed to get away and warn the local police. As a result there was no train crash and no ambush. The outlaws were about to be attacked by the full force of the police.

We shall probably never know what influenced Kelly's decision at this point. Was he in despair at the breakdown of his plan, was it in a spirit of resignation that he told his men, 'Now's the time to stand and fight!' Was it the Irishman's perennial love of a scrap—or did he genuinely believe he had a good chance of victory?

Whatever his reasoning, stand he did, as about thirty police made a direct attack on the Glenrowan Hotel. Kelly and his men put on their cast-iron armour—suits that weighed eighty pounds, helmets an additional sixteen pounds. So great was the weight that only Ned, with his great strength, could support the full outfit. The cumbersome gear hampered the wearer's movements and restricted his aim, but at the same time it was unquestionably bulletproof.

In fact of the direct attack, Ned's colleagues thought they should leave, but a prompt success—the wounding of the leader of the police attack, a man named Hare—encouraged their leader to fight it out. 'I've cooked old Hare, and we'll soon finish the rest. Cover me and I'll get round behind them and slaughter them from there.'

And so began the most macabre, the most courageous and the most memorable episode in the history of outlawry. Ned's sister Kate made a brave attempt to call off the siege; a trooper got close enough to the building to set it alight; and Ned himself moved slowly, cumbersomely forward to attack his attackers:

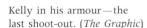
Kelly in his armour—the last shoot-out. (*The Graphic*)

The daring Kate Kelly came forth from the crowd
and on her poor brother she called out aloud:
'Come forth, my dear brother, and fight while you can!'
But a ball had just taken the life of poor Dan.

Next morning our hero came forth from the bush
encased in strong armour his way he did push.
To gain his bold comrades it was his desire—
the troopers espied him and soon opened fire.

The bullets bounced off him just like a stone wall,
his fiendish appearance soon did them appal.
His legs unprotected a trooper then found
and a shot well directed brought him to the ground.

The ballad's words sum up succinctly the course of events. Bullets thudded against Kelly's armour, powerless to wound but causing severe bruises with their impact. 'Fire away, you can't hurt me!' he is supposed to have shouted, and when they called on him to surrender, 'Never while I have a shot left.' But in the end, bruised all over and wounded in the leg, he was unable to fight on, and was taken. He was stripped of his armour and given medical treatment; none of the rest of his gang had survived, all had been shot or burned to death in the blazing hotel.

In prison they asked him why he had chosen to attack the police. 'A man gets tired of being hunted like a dog in his native land. I

Kelly in the prison hospital at Melbourne. (*The Graphic*)

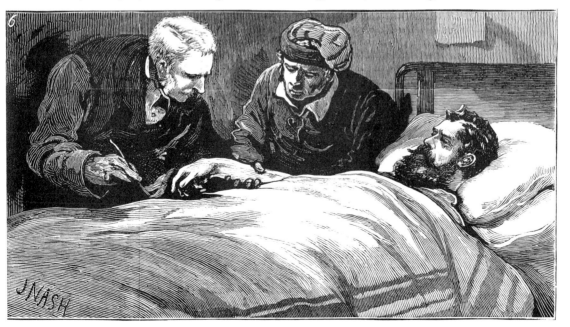

The execution of Ned Kelly at Melbourne, 11th November 1880.

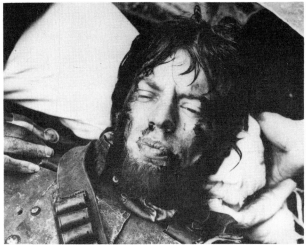

Mick Jagger in *Ned Kelly* a moving and perceptive film which came close to a true understanding of the highway robber and his motivations.

wanted to see the thing end.' Why had he advanced on the police in the end, when he might have tried to get away? 'A man would be a nice sort of dingo to walk out on his mates.'

Kelly was taken to Melbourne, a public hero despite the moralising of the ballads:

> Now you daring young fellows, take warning by me.
> Beware of bushranging and bad company.
> For, like many others, you may feel the dart
> which pierced the two Kellys, Joe Byrne and Steve Hart.

Kelly soon recovered from his wounds and stood trial for his many crimes. Inevitably he was sentenced to death. There were 60,000 signatures on the petition for a reprieve, but the authorities had been sorely tried by the Kelly Gang, and its leader was hanged on 11 November 1880. He was not the last of Australia's bushrangers, but he was unquestionably the greatest upholder of that tradition which had started to crystallise into legend more than half a century before:

> He fought six rounds with the horse police before the fatal
> > ball
> which pierced his heart and made him start, caused Donahoe
> > to fall.
> And then he closed his mournful eyes, his pistol an empty toy,
> crying 'Parents dear, O say a prayer for the Wild Colonial
> > Boy!'

9 Brothers in arms

The ghost of Sherwood Forest rode across the American plains and deserts, still pillaging the rich to give to the poor, still carrying the rebel's banner of the underdog rampant and triumphant.

(Robert Elman, Badmen of the West)

The picture of the American West as presented by Hollywood's Western movies is false only as it presents distorted images of the individual characters who created the history of the West. The background of general lawlessness and violence is not exaggerated, and the facts are there to bear the moviemakers out. But those facts are by no means as picturesque as the moviemakers make them look, nor are the characters who act out their stories against that background quite so colourful. The distortion arises not simply from the fact that legend has polarised them into an over-simplified black and white. The black was black alright, it's just that the white was never so white. There were no heroes in the American West, only different kinds of villain.

In Australia a man had to travel inland to escape from the restrictions of law and order; in America he had only to travel West. The new territories, from the Mexican border to the Canadian, offered the renegade a happier hunting ground than ever it had offered the Indian. For now added to the rich bounty with which nature covered the ground was the wealth she had hidden beneath it—gold and silver which teased men with the prospect of a faster, richer reward than even the luckiest hunter or most successful

140

Fugitive persued by the posse. (Frederick Remington in *The Century Magazine* 1888)

rancher could hope to get. And with the mining prospectors came the parasites—the saloon-keepers, the merchants and traders, the madams and their girls. All alike had to travel, and as they travelled they offered tempting pickings for the universal predator, the highwayman.

There were of course rich pickings in the city too. The streets of San Francisco were a midden of violence and corruption, teeming with opportunity for every known species of criminal. Sporadic attempts to impose law and order only highlighted the shortage of both these commodities; the rough justice of the vigilantes was only one step removed from the criminality they sought to curb; the lynch mobs superior to their victims only in the presumption of their claim to represent the right. But city crime is city crime the whole world over: San Francisco was worse than Chicago or New York only in that the ecological balance between law-breaker and law-enforcer had not yet been struck, so that anarchy still ruled its streets.

But the squalid opportunist anarchy of the urban jungle was not what the West was all about. What the West offered the criminal in unique abundance was space. Even though a township—a gold town or a cattle town—happened to have been 'tamed' by a tougher-than-average lawman with a solider-than-average backing from the citizens, there still remained a deal of empty space between it and the next town, and in that space the robber had a chance to fashion his life on his own terms—to rob, to make his getaway, to hide till supplies ran out and it was time to rob again. Small wonder, then, that the men who gave the West their bad names were the wide-ranging highwaymen of the stagecoach trails, not the squalid scavengers of the city streets.

Trails connected the towns—stagecoach trails, and sometimes railways. Both coaches and trains were vulnerable in their own way, and both were the constant target of the outlaw when he needed to replenish his funds. There was a limit to what he could obtain directly by brandishing his gun in the face of settlers and farmers; he needed cash to purchase supplies and to buy what security he could. Cash helped him obtain the co-operation, or at least the silence, of those who might otherwise have turned against him in hope of reward. For in this free-enterprise society of the new America, it was no longer enough to 'be a hero'. Here, a man had to make his own way and admiration was awarded for what a man did rather than what he was.

A claim for sympathy helped a little, no doubt. The most famous train-robber of them all, Jesse James, always claimed that he had taken to outlawry in consequence of the injustice he received at the termination of the Civil War, and while his argument is a Machiavellian twisting of the facts, there is a certain thread of logic in it. More credibly, the wretched plight of the Mexicans in America after the acquisition of California to some extent excuses their turning to crime, though it hardly justifies the violence with which they pursued their criminal careers.

Because of the element of logic in their positions, these people could exert sufficient emotional leverage to induce a certain sympathy among ordinary people. But what succeeded with the average citizen was not the hard-luck story—hard luck is equivalent to failure in the American ethos, and failure is equivalent to crime— what succeeded was success. It was Jesse James' skill and ruthlessness which made him a hero, his ability to use a gun and his readiness to display that ability—not any specious emotional plea.

Working for him, too, was that other fundamental trait in the American character, the tradition of being 'agin the government', of regarding the establishment as a natural oppressor. To the settler, Washington was one of the hostile forces of nature that had to be reckoned with along with the climate or the Indians. That independent pioneer spirit, which had inspired the original settlers to escape from government in Europe to freedom in America, and had then inspired them to escape from government in the Eastern states to freedom in the Western territories, was conducive to the highwayman's posture as a free-ranging authority-defying symbol of manly resolution and independence. He was the natural hero of those who believed, more than they believed anything else, that a man had a right to do his own thing and go his own way without interference. It wasn't quite what John Stuart Mill had in mind, but their brand of liberty was an ideology of a sort, even though it did give the James Brothers and the Younger Brothers and the Reno Brothers and the Dalton Brothers the opportunity to ride roughshod over the rest of humanity. It was a dilemma which Americans have had to face in a sharper form than other peoples; it is a dilemma which they have yet to resolve. In the meantime:

The man who held up a train, a gold-laden stagecoach, or a bank, was seen as a Robin Hood, even though he forgot to share the loot.
                                        (*Robert Elman, Badmen of the West*)

America has possessed robbers and outlaws from the moment there was anything to rob or a law to be outside. One of the passengers on the *Mayflower* was hanged in 1630, though that was for murder rather than robbery. The English Highwayman had his transatlantic emulators in 18th century America, lone robbers operating along the highways of New England just as Turpin and Rann were doing back in old England.

But the characteristic form of highway robbery in America was to be the gang. It was a process logically dictated by the nature of the quarry. For if the violent independence of the American West was favourable to the breeding of outlaws, it also bred men ready to defend their property with their guns in a way which was exceptional in Europe or even Australia. American stagecoaches were armed to an extent never known in England and a sizeable gang was usually considered necessary to ensure success when robbing a stagecoach. A few lone highwaymen made a success of their trade — Black Bart of California had a prefeence for working alone which made him one of the most truly heroic, as well as one of the most mysterious of the badmen; but most of the big names of the West are the names of gangs or leaders of gangs.

The pattern was set as early as the time of the Revolutionary War, when the Doane Gang, cloaking their activities under the guise of loyalist action, carried out a series of violent robberies purporting to be on behalf of the British cause. The proceeds went more frequently into their own pockets and when they continued their activities after the war, the new government moved decisively against them. Throughout the years 1787 and 1788 they were harried and pursued, and one by one were caught and hanged.

To document fully the robbery of stagecoaches and trains in the American West would be a tiresome job and make tedious reading but the ultimate statistics would be fascinating. It is clear that robbing the stage was literally an everyday affair—that every day, on this trail or that, some highwayman was holding up some stage-coach. Certain places during certain periods were particularly hard hit: at Deadwood, during the Black Hills Gold Rush of the 1870s, the stages were held up every few days. The robbers, largely consisting of unsuccessful prospectors made desperate by failure, took back with interest what they had paid out to the extortionate saloon-keepers, madams and traders who were themselves exploiting the miners.

There were no trains from Deadwood and, even if there had been, the banks' and merchants' consignments would hardly have been safer. Train robberies, too, were almost an everyday occurrence, so frequent that the names of half the perpetrators remain unrecorded. In November 1870, $40,000 was taken from the Wells Fargo box on a Central Pacific train at Verdi, Nevada, by a gambler named Parsons and a businessman named Davis; they were caught soon after the robbery. But the following day, the same train was robbed again; this time a little farther down the line. The names of the robbers are unknown today and, perhaps, were not even known at the time—it was just another train robbery.

The first train robbery recorded in America was immediately after the end of the Civil War, when the Reno Brothers flagged down a train near Seymour, Indiana, boarded it at gunpoint, and got away with $10,000. That day's work set a pattern for generations of train robbers, whose activities did not finally cease until well into the following century.

Frank Reno.

The Mexicans

The not-too-well-known American poet Cincinnatus Heine Miller (1839–1913) was presumably given those baptismal names because of his parents' admiration for two great men, but he himself, in later years, preferred to style himself Joaquin Miller, in honour of one of the Mexican horse-thieves with whom he rode the Californian deserts in the 1850s. Referring to the annexation of California by the United States in 1848 after the war with Mexico, he wrote:

After the cruel conquest of California from Mexico, we poured in upon the simple and hospitable people, from all parts of the United States. Strangers in language and religion, let it be honestly admitted, we were often guilty of gross wrong to the conquered Californians. Out of this wrong suddenly sprang Joaquin Murieta, a mere boy, and yet one of the boldest men in history. But he soon degenerated into a robber and a large reward was

offered for his head. The splendid daring and unhappy death of this
remarkable youth appeal strongly to me—and, bandit as he was, I am
bound to say I have a great respect for his memory.

At the age of nineteen, Murieta went to work in California as a miner.
He was forced to leave by a gang of whites who insisted that 'no
damned Mexican had a right to work in an American mine'; he was
beaten up and his sweetheart outraged. He then tried to work as a
farmer, and again was forced to quit. Soon he was accused of horse
thieving; when he called his half-brother as a witness to his
innocence, the latter was lynched and he himself was whipped
nearly to death. Kneeling over the body of his murdered brother, he
swore that he would devote the rest of his life to avenging the crime.
Then he set to work systematically to kill each of the band who had
lynched his brother.

But he wanted more than simple retribution. In 1850 he formed a
gang who waged a fierce campaign of robbery with murder. Because
he represented the cause of the oppressed Mexican inhabitants of
California, he had no difficulty in obtaining supplies and support
from his compatriots; his promise to protect those who befriended
him, and his threat of death to those who betrayed him, were both
carried out with impressive punctiliousness, and helped to increase
the respect, if not the affection, in which he was held. So supplies,
arms and information—the necessities of the bandit's trade—were
always forthcoming.

The number of crimes committed by the Murieta gang will probably never be known, because almost every robbery in California was credited to them whether or not they were genuinely responsible. Throughout 1851, travellers and farms were robbed all over the territory, while horse trading provided a steady income. The gang numbered some seventy members in 1852; often the men's mistresses would ride with the robbers, wearing men's clothing. Soon Murieta was a legend—a patriotic legend for the Mexicans, a terrible bogey for the white settlers. He began to attract the customary anecdotes. His courtesy to women was emphasised— when his gang captured a girl in the course of a robbery and were preparing to rape her, Murieta is said to have prevented them and let her go.

He had a near escape in 1852 when he was caught stealing horses by a tribe of local Indians. Word was sent to the authorities but they, not realising who had been caught, and not bothering to concern themselves with quarrels between one crowd of natives and another, told the Indian chief to deal with the matter any way he wanted. So Murieta, after a whipping from his captors, escaped to rob again. Soon after this he learned that Deputy Sheriff Wilson of Santa Barbara County had been boasting of what he would do to Murieta when he laid hands on him. Murieta disguised himself, rode into Los Angeles, sought out someone who could point Wilson out to him, rode up to him as he stood on the sidewalk with a group of companions, whispered something in his ear, drew his gun and shot him through the head. In July 1852, hearing that Major General Joshua Bean was organising a large posse to come after him, Murieta staged an ambush and stabbed the general to death.

At this time it was estimated that his attacks on gold shipments alone had netted him $50,000. There were now said to be ninety men in his gang and twenty five women—a small army against which no ordinary posse would stand a chance, however efficiently it was organised and however well it knew the country. The only hope of the authorities was betrayal, and even with a $5000 reward on Murieta's head there was no great hope of that, so strong was his hold on the loyalty of his fellow countrymen. That hold was strengthened by such incidents as occurred in April 1853, when another posse received a tip-off as to where Murieta was sleeping. A surprise attack was carried out; Murieta was surrounded and barely managed to escape. Only a few members of the posse knew who had supplied the information, yet next morning the informer was found hanged.

Naturally, Murieta could not always move with his entire force, if for no other reason than that the supply problem became too great.

The authorities' best hope, therefore, was to come up against the bandit when he was in a relatively small party, and so it was when a company of Mounted Rangers, under Captain Harry Love, finally located Murieta's secret camp and attacked it shortly after sunrise on the morning of 25 July 1853. Murieta himself was washing his horse; he leapt onto its back and tried to get away, shouting to his companions to do the same. But his mare was shot and he himself was thrown to the ground. He picked himself up and tried to run, but was quickly riddled with bullets. He turned towards the posse, threw up his hands and cried, 'Don't shoot any more, boys, the work is done'—then fell without another word.

Love rode back to the city with Murieta's head as proof of his success—needed if he was to claim the $6000 reward—and, for good measure, the hand of his partner, Three-Finger Jake; more certain proof of identity than his head. Murieta's head was displayed at King's Saloon in San Francisco, and a tradition of bad luck accompanied it thereafter. King himself went bankrupt, and the head passed to Deputy Sheriff Harrison who sold it to a gunsmith named Natchez. Harrison committed suicide and Natchez was killed in a pistol accident. As for Love himself, he was shot by his wife's bodyguard in a mysterious incident in 1868. It could, of course, be argued that in that violent part of the world during that violent period, such deaths were by no means out of the way, but it added a piquant postscript to the Murieta legend.

There were many who claimed that the man Love killed was not Murieta at all, and stories about his deeds continued to circulate, though it is more likely that others assumed his name out of admiration or bravado. At the time of his death, Murieta had been working out a plan to recruit a small army of five hundred Mexicans who would sweep through the whole of California in one glorious final rampage, robbing as they went and killing off all those against whom they had scores to settle, and then move on into Mexico and disband. The fact that nothing more was ever heard of this grand scheme supports the view that it really was Murieta that Love killed.

But Murieta's death by no means ended the conflict between Mexican outlaws and the Californian authorities. Juan Soto, Noratto Ponce, Narciso Bojorques, Antonio Garcia, Tiburcio Vasquez, Cleovara Chavez—each in turn, over the ensuing fifteen years, assumed the leadership of the outlaw band and enjoyed a brief career of fame. Bojorques was killed in a saloon fight in 1865 by an American bandit named One-Eyed Jack; in the same year Ponce was gunned down in the course of a running fight with Sheriff Harry Morse, who was also responsible for slaying Juan Soto six years later. Garcia was captured and hanged for murdering a police

Cole Younger immediately after his capture.

Tiburcio Vasquez, Mexican bandit in California. (Duke, *Celebrated Criminal cases of America*)

John Younger.

Frank James.

Bob Younger, two weeks before recieving his fatal wound, 1889.

Jim Younger in 1889.

Jesse James in 1860.

constable. Vasquez, perhaps Murieta's most celebrated successor, had a reward of $8000 alive, $6000 dead on his head when he was caught in a trap in 1874 and hanged at San José. Bounty-hunters, too, were responsible for the shooting down of Chavez, last of the great names among the Mexican bandits of California. They were, perhaps, the most ruthless set of highwaymen to be described in our pages, never hesitating to kill, never failing in courage, but it was the courage and ruthlessness of desperate men, driven by injustice to defy justice. As something approaching law and order came to the West, their cause lost its emotional force and their way of life its impetus, and soon their day was done.

The Younger Brothers and the James Brothers

The interwoven histories of these two families form the most eventful and extended saga in the history of the Western badmen. Cole Younger, who was born in 1844, and Frank James, born a year later, had both been members of Quantrell's Marauders, a free-ranging troop of horsemen who purportedly supported the Confederate cause during the Civil War. Beneath the cloak of patriotic guerilla operations they in fact waged what was no better than a private war on their own behalf. Their force of four hundred and fifty men acquired an appalling reputation for savagery in their attacks on anyone who opposed the Southern cause. It is true that, to combat their ruthless methods, the Northern forces also resorted to methods hardly less savage, but it seems clear enough that it was Quantrell and his men who called the tune to which all had to dance; even the Confederate government, desperate though its plight, disowned the Marauders.

After Quantrell's death the force continued its activities under 'Bloody' Bill Anderson. When the South finally surrendered, it was announced that criminal proceedings would be taken against all who had ridden with Quantrell and Anderson. Rather than take their chance in court at a time when emotions were running so high, Cole Younger and his younger brothers Jim (born in 1848) and Bob (born in 1853) decided to head for the West. Claiming that the Federal authorities had murdered their father, a respectable judge, and were responsible for the accidental death of three of their sisters, the Youngers took a Black Oath of vengeance. Undoubtedly there was some justice in their claim, but not sufficient to warrant their decision to wage eternal war on their former enemies.

When he failed to turn up for his trial in 1866, Cole Younger was officially declared an outlaw and so was Frank James who now, with

Holding up the pay escort. (Remington in *Harpers Monthly* 1895)

The Younger brothers hold up the Missouri Pacific railroad at Rocky Cut, (T. H. Robinson in Griffiths, *Mysteries of Police and Crime*)

"HOLDING UP" A TRAIN ON THE MISSOURI PACIFIC RAILWAY (p. 335).

his younger brother Jesse, joined the three Youngers and agreed to work with them. Their first operation, carried out that same year, was a raid on the bank at Liberty, Missouri, which netted them some $15,000 in gold. It was the first of at least two dozen such raids carried out over the next sixteen years, together with any number of smaller operations. In the course of these activities, they killed at least ten people for certain, and probably a great many more. It became the custom to credit them with many crimes for which they were not in fact responsible, so the degree of their guilt isn't easy to establish. Between operations they maintained a low profile, which serves to explain the length of their criminal careers. Aiding them, too, was the goodwill of neighbours in their own country who, whether from genuine sympathy or from self-interest, helped the robbers by their silence, if not by more positive proofs of loyalty.

While bank raiding was always the most lucrative form of

150

robbery, it was also by far the most dangerous, for the citizens of a township had a direct interest in the welfare of the bank, and taking on a bank could mean taking on an entire community. To attack a stagecoach or a train was a safer bet, giving the robbers the choice of location and allowing them to plan their getaway in advance. Train robbing became a speciality of the Younger/James gang. Their attack on the Chicago, Rock Island and Pacific Railroad train at Adair, Iowa, in July 1873, was a typical enterprise. They started by wrecking the train, in preference to holding it up: on this occasion the driver was killed and several passengers injured, but the general effect was to shake up the passengers so severely that it drove all thoughts of resistance from their minds. All the gang got from this particular robbery was $3000 in cash and such valuables as they could find in the passengers' possession. Encouraged by the reward, hundreds of men volunteered to take part in the pursuit, but all their efforts were in vain, thanks to the refusal of the outlaws' countrymen to give information to the authorities. Already the gangsters, and Jesse James in particular, were acquiring the status of heroes: it was said of Jesse that he never robbed a friend, nor a preacher, nor a Southerner, nor a widow.

Stagecoaches continued to be rewarding targets: in 1874 they took $4000 from the Hot Springs coach. But they did better still from their next railroad robbery, later the same year, when they took over the station at Gadshill—by coincidence, the name of a celebrated highwaymen's resort in England—and held up the next train. They

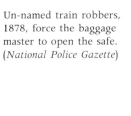

Un-named train robbers, 1878, force the baggage master to open the safe. (*National Police Gazette*)

A fight in the street.
(Remington, *Century Magazine* 1888)

then proceeded to loot it systematically, working their way through the coaches robbing each individual traveller, and ending up with $10,000 in cash and $3400 in jewelry. The authorities increased the rewards and called in Pinkerton's Detective Agency, while many bounty hunters went into business on their own behalf. In an ambush which came near to ending the careers of the outlaws, John Younger was killed and Jim wounded.

In March 1875 the Missouri state legislature tried to introduce an Outlaw Amnesty Bill. This provided a pardon for all crimes committed under the Confederate banner, if the James and Youngers would submit to stand trial for their activities since the war. But before the outlaws could decide one way or the other, public opinion had quashed the proposal. From a sociological viewpoint, it is interesting to notice the way the pendulum of sympathy swung now for, now against the outlaws. Initially there had been a considerable sympathy for them, partly because of a genuine belief that the brothers had had a raw deal, and partly from solidarity with the Southern cause. Then, as citizens found themselves suffering from the robberies on their banks and money shipments, and because local people were often the victims of the rail and coach hold-ups, sympathy swung away. When, in January 1875, a home-made bomb was hurled by an over-eager bounty-hunter through the window of a house belonging to the James family, though none of the outlaws was in fact there at the time, killing the nine year old half-brother of the outlaws and blowing off their mother's arm, a wave of fresh sympathy was aroused, only to die again as the incident faded in people's minds and new outrages by the gangsters took its place.

In the same year, at Muncie in Kansas, $55,000 was taken in the course of a single attack. Many more banks were raided. In 1876 they took $17,000 from a Missouri Pacific train at Rocky Cut, in the course of a leisurely seventy-minute stroll through the coaches. But on 7th September of the same year they backed their own luck once too often. In the course of a raid on the First National Bank at Northfield, Minnesota, the brothers found themselves opposed by an unusually vigorous force of citizens. Three of the eight members of the gang were killed, and two of the Younger brothers were wounded before they got safely away from the town. With the posse hard on their heels, Jim Younger's serious wounds endangered them all. Jesse was all for finishing him off, saying that he couldn't live anyway. His brothers disagreed, and the two families agreed to separate. Riding for their lives through the rain, wounded, with no chance to sleep and no food to sustain them, the Youngers were an easy prey despite their knowledge of the countryside; after a desperate struggle they were cornered and taken alive.

In prison, public sympathy turned in their favour, particularly when their seventeen year old sister Reta joined them there. They pleaded guilty: depite their many killings, this did not necessarily incur the death penalty, and all three brothers were sentenced to terms of imprisonment. They were good prisoners. Bob died of tuberculosis in 1889, but the others were paroled in 1901. Jim Younger tried his hand as a salesman, but was unable to adapt to normal life and killed himself a few months later. Cole Younger travelled the country giving lectures on the evils of crime. His moral was, 'The man who chooses a career of outlawry is either a natural fool or an innocent madman'. He lived until 1916.

Meanwhile Frank and Jesse James had escaped into Mexico, where, for a while, they kept themselves alive by rustling cattle over the border. In 1879 they returned to America and once again turned to train robbery. At Glendale, on the Chicago, Alton and St Louis Railway, near Kansas City, they took a rich haul of $35,000. In September 1880 they held up eight wealthy tourists visiting the Mammoth Cave in Kentucky, and got away with $1500 and their jewelry. For the next nine years they kept clear of the law, carrying out all kinds of robbery in different locations, until the Governor of Misouri was driven to offer a state reward of $10,000 dead or alive.

With such a reward over a man's head, it was only a matter of time before someone decided that it was worth risking the reprisals when so large a sum could be won just for shooting a man. And so it came about; in April 1890 Jesse James was shot in the back by a colleague named Robert Ford, who had been pretending to plan a bank raid with Jesse but had a personal grudge against him. And so the most notorious of the Western badmen was killed; not in some spectacular ambush or shoot-out; not in one of his daring bank raids or railroad hold-ups, but while standing on a stool to hang a picture on the wall of his sitting room.

Six months later his brother Frank gave himself up, declaring that he was tired of being hunted for more than twenty years. He was put on trial for murder, but no sure evidence was forthcoming and he was released. One of his reasons for giving himself up was that he believed himself to be dying of consumption, but in the event he lived another quarter of a century, farming the land where his little half-brother had been killed, and giving occasional lectures, like Cole Younger, on the evils of the highwayman's life.

Charles Bolton ('Black Bart')

The highwayman known as 'Black Bart' came closer to the traditional English model than any of his American brothers in arms, with one notable difference—he was a relatively old man of fifty seven.

In the year 1877 he took $325 off the stagecoach at Fort Ross, near Russian River. On this, his first venture, as throughout his career, he operated on his own, masked, and cloaked from head to foot in a white sheet-like garment which provided an effective disguise against identification. He was armed with a shotgun, but neither then nor on any subsequent occasion was he known to use it. He insisted later that it was never even loaded.

After his second robbery, on 28 July 1878, when he took $600 from the Quincy to Oroville coach, he left these lines handwritten on the waybill, addressed to the Wells Fargo company:

Charles Bolton, or Boles, better known as 'Black Bart'.

> Here I lay me down to sleep
> to wait the coming morrow.
> Perhaps success, perhaps defeat
> and everlasting sorrow.

Yet come what will, I'll try it on—
my condition can't be worse.
And if there's money in that box,
'tis money in my purse.

Because there had been mail involved in the second robbery, his offence was a Federal matter, and a large reward was offered. But Black Bart was the most elusive of highwaymen, and continued his career unmolested, giving no clue to would-be pursuers. His targets were always stagecoaches on the less frequented Californian trails— the Covelo to Ukiah stage, the Weaverville to Shasta stage—twenty eight of them until an unfortunate accident, together with some astute detective work, brought his criminal career to a close.

In 1883 Black Bart robbed the Milton to Sonora coach, which was carrying the driver only, no passengers. While opening the box, the highwayman cut his hand, and used his handkerchief as a bandage. While he was helping himself to the $550 in coin and $4100 in amalgam that the coach was carrying, another traveller came up the trail. Black Bart prudently made a run for it, but the driver of the coach seized the newcomer's gun and fired a shot at the fleeing robber. He missed, but in the confusion Black Bart dropped his handkerchief-bandage.

Trivial as it was, it was the clue the police needed. They found a laundry mark on the handkerchief, which suggested that he was a town dweller, for a countryman would wash his linen by hand. So the mark was checked in the laundries of San Francisco and, ultimately, it was discovered that F.O.X.7 was a mining engineer named Bolton who, his landlady acknowledged, frequently went away on survey trips into the hills.

Bolton himself was an immaculately dressed, courteous middle-aged gentleman. At first he denied the charges completely; then, confronted by the evidence against him, he graciously admitted. He pleaded guilty to the Sonora robbery and obligingly showed the police where the loot was stashed. In November 1883 he was sent to San Quentin Goal for a seven year stretch, but was released after four years thanks to his good behaviour. He promised that he would commit no further crimes. When asked if he would compose any more verses, he said, 'Didn't you hear me say I would commit no more crimes?' From that day Black Bart was never heard of again, though there were rumours that he had taken to farming in Nevada.

Charles Dorsey

In the same year that Black Bart walked out of San Quentin gaol, another highwayman successfully escaped over its walls. This was Charles Dorsey, not one of the 'big names' in Western history, but perhaps for that reason more typical than some of the men who carried out the greater number of the robberies—for, despite their reputation, the Youngers' and the James' and the Daltons' were responsible for only a tiny fraction of the robberies committed in the West.

Dorsey and a colleague John Patterson stopped the Eureka stage at Moore's Flat, near Nevada City, on September 1st 1879. One man held the passengers covered with his gun while the other searched the coach. When Patterson pulled out a case from beneath the passengers' seat and opened it to find a gold bar worth $6700, its owner, a banker named William Cummings, tried to resist. In the momentary panic, Dorsey, covering with his gun, shot the banker dead.

For the time being the two robbers got away. Then, some three years later, Patterson was caught by the St Louis police and held for trial on a burglary charge. An informer told the San Francisco police that Patterson had been one of the Moore's Flat robbers. He was brought to California, tried and convicted, and hanged at Nevada City in February 1884. Further information put the police on the trail of his confederate. He was discovered in Union City, Indiana, where he had started a wood merchant's business under the name of Moore—choosing the name as an ironic tribute to the source of his initial capital. He was such a popular member of the community that mob violence was threatened when the police came to arrest him. However, he was taken to San Francisco, tried and convicted. While awaiting execution at San Quentin in 1887 he managed to escape; three years later he was recaptured in Chicago.

George Sontag.

John & George Sontag and Chris Evans

To many of the settlers in the American West, the railroads were the most palpable symbol of authority; powerful, and using their power ruthlessly, they came to represent the impersonal establishment against which it was the moral duty of the free man to defend himself. The hard bargains they drove when they needed a settler's land, the strong-arm methods they used to get their way, endeared them to none, even when their traffic was not a direct threat to local interests. So robbing the railroads was hardly considered a crime,

156

John Sontag.

Chris Evans.

even when there was no other justification.

As it happens, two of the Sontag-Evans gang believed they did have further justification. John Sontag, born in 1861, reckoned that he had been unjustly treated by his old employers, the Southern Pacific Railroad, when he had been injured at work. He met Chris Evans, who also bore some grudge against the railroads, and they determined to be revenged. On January 21st, 1889, they boarded a train near Goshen, California. Their methods were the classic ones: with masks on their faces and guns in their hands, they climbed over the tender and forced the engineer to halt the train, then made their way to the Express Car and took some $600 from the safe. They then escaped on the horses standing ready for them. A month later, at Pixley, they carried out a similar raid; this time they were luckier, and took $5000.

At this point they enslisted the help of George Sontag, John's brother. In 1891 the three of them robbed the Chicago train on the Pacific line, and took just under $10,000. Further raids brought in more proceeds, and by now the prosperity of the three men was attracting the suspicion of the authorities. The police paid them a visit; they panicked and shooting broke out. One policeman was killed; two more were shot in a further shoot-out before George was captured in 1892 and sent to Folsom prison for life.

Chris Evans and John Sontag continued to be sheltered by local folk who believed they had a genuine grievance. Ultimately, however, the police caught up with the fugitives: Chris Evans was captured in June 1893 after being wounded in a gunfight, and, after a long drawn out pursuit, John Sontag was gunned down in the San Joaquin Valley. On hearing the news of his brother's death, George tried to escape from prison and was shot in the process. Chris Evans also made an escape bid and managed to elude the police for two months before recapture. A popular melodrama of the day, *Sontag and Evans*, presented the three robbers as heroes, courageously defying the power of the wicked railroads and their police stooges.

Browning and Brady

In the year 1896 detectives working for Wells Fargo heard a story which just might tie in with one of their most fruitless inquiries. A hobo named Carl the Tramp, who until October 1894 hadn't had a cent in the world, seemed suddenly to have struck it rich. For the past two years he had been living on a scale which suggested an inexhaustible supply of funds—gambling, drinking, eating at the best restaurants and patronising the most expensive women. The

Samuel Browning.

John Brady.

detectives carefully worked their way into his confidence, and eventually learned the explanation. Two years before, while sleeping in a ditch near Sacramento, California, he had found a huge cache of money. He had made off with as much as he could carry in a single load, but feared to go back for the rest in case he should be spotted by the people—presumably desperate criminals—who had hidden it there. He had secured $33,000 and in the past two years had already managed to spend $21,000 of it.

It was clear to the detectives that the $33,000 was part of the missing $53,000 taken from a Wells Fargo safe on the No 3 Omaha Overland on 12 October 1894. The two robbers, who were clearly familiar with railroad operating methods, had stolen dynamite cartridges of the type used for signalling trains, and a red lantern was taken from a track-walker. With these they had stopped the Omaha Overland which left San Francisco at 6pm, at a convenient location near Davisville, California. The engineer and fireman of the halted train were ordered at pistol point to the third car back, the Wells Fargo car, and this car was uncoupled and the train separated front and rear. The engineer was instructed to persuade the Fargo man to open up or he himself would be shot. Some futile shooting took place by way of protest, then the guard opened up, and the robbers took the $53,000 to the locomotive, carried by the railwaymen. They then boarded the locomotive, drove it for three miles, took off the loot, put the engine into reverse and sent it back along the tracks, unmanned, to rejoin the train—as steam was running low by now, the damage was only slight.

It had all been a meticulously planned robbery, and the planning had paid off. If it hadn't been for the lucky discovery of Carl the Tramp, the unknown robbers would have got away with one of the biggest hauls in train-robbing history. Police and rail detectives worked together, but in vain.

Perhaps because they had secured only a fraction of the take from the previous robbery, the two men decided on a similar operation the following spring. On 30 March 1895 the Oregon Express No 15, was stopped in the same fashion near Maryville. This time, though, the safe was a combination one, and there was no means of opening it. The robbers decided to take what they could get from the passengers but a sheriff happened to be travelling on the train, and decided to make some attempt at resistance. In the ensuing gunfight the sheriff was killed but so was one of the bandits. He was identified as Samuel Browning of San Francisco, and his partner, who had got away successfully, as John Brady. For some months there was no sign of Brady, then he was spotted, caught, tried and sentenced to life imprisonment for robbery and shooting. History does not record the subsequent career of Carl, the world's luckiest tramp.

The Dalton Brothers

Ben, Frank, Grattan, William, Robert and Emmet Dalton were not only named after famous Irishmen, they were related to the hardly less famous Younger brothers—their mother was the Youngers' father's sister. Settled in Cherokee territory, they were fundamentally as respectable as most folk in that part of the world—one brother was even a deputy marshal—but their fringe activities gradually took them over to the wrong side of the law. When a

159

Grattan Dalton.

Bob Dalton.

An attack on the Great Northern Line, near Seattle: blowing up the Express car with dynamite. $5000 was gained, but the sheriff's posse took them all after a shoot-out. (*Le Petit Parisien*)

warrant for horse thieving was taken out against Bob and Grattan, the two brothers joined a gang of outlaws.

From horse stealing their activities came to be more specifically directed against that universal enemy of the settler, the Southern Pacific Railroad. Anyone who opposed the railroads and their land-grabbing operations was automatically a local hero and Bill Dalton, at this time a respectable citizen and an ambitious politician, was vigorously concerned to protect the community from the railroad men. But his kinship with the notorious Youngers told against him, and enabled his political opponents to suggest that his motives were not so high-minded as he wanted folk to think. When some train robberies were committed in the neighbourhood in 1891, they were credited to the Daltons, and Bill was arrested on suspicion by some hopeful contestant for the $6000 reward. He was able to prove his innocence but Grattan, less confident of aquittal, escaped from gaol to join Emmet and Bob whose view was that, if people were going to blame them for robbing trains anyway, they may as well enjoy the fruits of the robbery. For the time being Bill, though his political ambitions were harmed by the association, continued to try to make an honest living.

In May 1891 Bob, Grattan and Emmet, with other colleagues from outside the family, attacked the Atchison, Topeka and Sante Fe railroad at Wharton in the Cherokee Strip, and took $14,000. Later the same year they took $19,000 in a similar raid at Lillietta. In 1892 there was a successful raid at Red Rock Station, but it brought them only $1800, and in October they came up against serious resistance at Adair and had to shoot their way to freedom. Perhaps this experience, together with the reasoning that banks were where the money was, led them to turn from moving targets to a stationary one. In October 1892 they went into action against two banks simultaneously at Coffeyville, Kansas: it seems that they were deliberately setting out to achieve a robbery which would bring them lasting fame, for Bob Dalton was heard to boast that it was a bigger thing than anything the James and Younger brothers had ever tried.

The success at Coffeyville aroused greater public spirit than their cousins' activities, perhaps less because of the scale of the operation than because times were changing. It was the 1890s now, and the Civil War had been over for more than a quarter of a century; law and order were coming to the West, and the old lawless independence was no longer tolerable. Pursuit led to a shoot-out in which Bob and Grattan were killed, while Emmet was badly wounded and captured. He was imprisoned, paroled after fourteen years and lived astonishingly until 1937.

160

But that was not the end of the Daltons. Their brother Bill, his political ambitions thwarted, now formed a bigger-than-ever outfit with his brothers Frank and Ben. For a time, thanks to local support from those who supplied them with food, drink, ammunition and other necessaries of life, the Daltons were able to continue their career without incident. But by now there were many bounty-hunters as well as official detectives on their trail, and each raid gave fresh impetus to their pursuers. The gang was forced to split, its members were shot down or captured one by one. Finally, in a shoot-out in 1894, Bill Dalton was surrounded by a posse in a farmhouse near Ardmore, and was gunned down while trying to escape.

The Wild Bunch

The end of the Dalton's career was not, however, the end of train robbery in the American West. It continued to be a lucrative activity, and was a speciality of the Hole in the Wall Gang in the 1890s who, as it were, took on the mantle of the Daltons. From a well-hidden and well-nigh impregnable base in the hills near Buffalo, Wyoming, which gave them their popular name, they sortied out under their leaders Kid Curry and Harry Longbaugh, better known as the Sundance Kid.

At the same time a similar gang was operating under the leadership of George Leroy Parker, also better known under his working name of Butch Cassidy. He had already acquired something of a reputation for courtesy in a line of business where such trimmings were rare; the legend went that on his first train hold-up, back in Colorado in 1887, Cassidy, on being told that the express-guards would not co-operate, refused to rob the passengers and rode off without taking a cent. Such stories contributed to the Butch Cassidy legend, but lack the ring of conviction; it seems more probable that the outlaw had a case of cold feet.

By 1897 the neighbourhood of the Hole in the Wall had become so infested with lawmen and bounty hunters that the gang decided to break out. Of its hundred or so members, a good many teamed up with Cassidy, forming the Wild Bunch which continued operations until well into the twentieth century. But though raids were continually being carried out, the rewards were small; the outlaws were continually on the run, in perpetual fear of their pursuers. In 1903 Cassidy and Longbaugh determined to try fresh fields, and with the proceeds of a successful raid on the bank at Winnemucca, set out for Argentina. For a while they tried to live honestly, but

Bandits rob passengers on the Rocky Mountain Express near Mudock, 1907. (*Le Petit Parisien*)

whether because their funds ran low, or because they could not resist trying their old ways, or because such had been their intention all along, they went back to train robbery. In 1909 they were cornered and gunned down by the Bolivian army — middle aged and desperate, the last of the great train robbers of the West.

As with so many of their predecessors from Robin Hood on, the killing was denied and the claim made that the pair 'returned to the U.S. and lived to a ripe old age'. The evidence makes this claim dubious. It seems far more probable, in the light of what we have learnt, that this is the old myth-making process at work again. But let it be so; if the world wants its highwaymen to survive, the legend obligingly keeps them alive. For those who prefer their tale to be rounded off with a ritual death, there is a version for them too—the hard-pressed fight, the hoped-for refuge, the realization of ambush, the final shoot out in the village square in the brave but hopeless dawn.

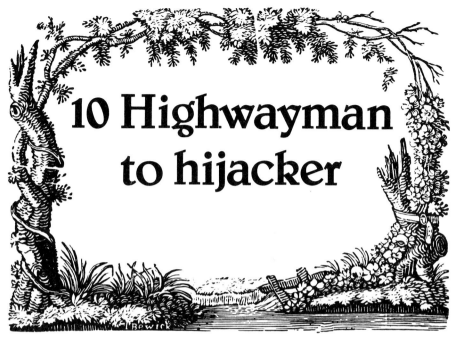

10 Highwayman to hijacker

Every criminal is an opportunist, responding to situations which present him with a chance to take advantage. Most often it's a simple seizing of advantage over his fellow men—taking their property while they are asleep, or winning their confidence with lies in order to cheat them. Sometimes the criminal is able to exploit a specific defect in the social structure—as when, for instance, man-made laws seek to prohibit gambling or alcoholic drink and so come into conflict with man's love of these things.

The highwayman is basically a thief who specialises in robbing travellers the way other thieves specialise in burgling houses or snatching payrolls. But at the same time, as we have seen, social factors have contrived to cast him for a larger, more significant role; seen him, despite his criminality, as the personification of an ideal. We must not let the fancy-dress get-up of the Christmas-supplement Highwayman, cloak, cocked hat and jingling spurs, distract us from the more meaningful myth which lies beneath. The wide open spaces of the legend, the galloping horses, the courage and the panache, are the outward trappings of something deeper—of overweening authority challenged, of ever-encroaching officialdom defied.

So the highwayman confronts us with a paradox: a social outcast chosen by society to perform a social role. Why him? Well, it has to be a criminal of some kind, because it must be someone who not only voices his dissent but proves it by the way of life he chooses and, of all social outcasts, the highwayman is the one who flaunts his opposition to society most bravely. So, whether he seeks it or not

Salvatore Giuliano outside
his mountain hideout.

(and he generally does) and whether he deserves it or not (and he
generally doesn't) the highwayman has usually managed to enjoy
more than his fair share of sympathy, popularity, and even
admiration.

On a purely material level, the highwayman can operate only
when he enjoys a certain freedom of manoeuvre; on a deeper level,
he must be able to count on a particular, and rather primitive, social
attitude to law and order which likewise allows him a measure of
freedom in which to operate. But what happens when conditions
change, when these freedoms are curtailed, when the open spaces
are no longer so wide, when the horse is no longer a viable means of
transport, when cocked hat and spurs are no longer the fashion, and
when public attitudes to authority are no longer so naïve?

As far as he can, of course, he simply adapts. The Sicilian bandit Salvatore Giuliano, who flourished in the 1950s, was a simple modification of the traditional Italian bandit, altering the old life-style only so far as was necessary to keep pace with modern developments. He was born in 1922 in the Montelepre district of Sicily, an area which also gave birth to the most notorious of American racketeers, Al Capone. Today aeroplanes fly overhead and bring parties of tourists to the towns; at election times communists and democrats wrestle for the right to govern the country; law and order are maintained by a force equipped with all the technology learnt in two world wars. Yet life off the main roads in Sicily remains one of astonishing barbarity, and Giuliano grew up in a community hardly changed from that which had produced generations of authority-defying bandits in the past.

In September 1943, when Giuliano was aged twenty, he was stopped by the Carabinieri while carrying a load of stolen flour on the back of a stolen mule. He defended himself with his gun, shot one policeman dead, and made his escape. He had taken the step across the line—he had killed his first policeman—there was nothing for it now but to become an outlaw.

There was nothing unusual about that—it was hardly more out of the way than any other occupation. All over Italy it was considered almost a virtue to be against the government. In Sicily, so far from Rome and so independent in spirit, it was a natural state of mind.

When Giuliano took to the hills, he found them full of outlaws like himself, men who in one way or another had run foul of the law. He was taken on by the Mafia as a 'rent collector'; before long he had made himself leader of a small gang and was in business for himself. Small successes led to larger ones, and success attracted others to join his band until he was leading a force of some fifty men, highly organised, trained, obedient, disciplined and loyal. Crime paid well. By kidnapping for ransom, by extortion and blackmail, and by simple robbery, Giuliano took an estimated £500,000 in the course of his career.

A good part of this—perhaps half—went on expenses: fifty men take a lot of feeding, there are arms and ammunition to buy, there are officials to be bribed. Once in a while, too, a well publicised and judiciously selected act of charity helped to win sympathy—so in the legend of Salvatore Giuliano, as in so many others, it is told how he robbed the wealthy to give to the poor.

Without the sympathy and support of the peasants, he and his men could not have survived for more than a few weeks. He needed to be able to move about the country in the secure knowledge—the *certainty*—that, whether through love or fear, no ordinary citizen would dare to betray his movements to the authorities. And this certainty Giuliano enjoyed, to the extent that he could even venture into towns and villages where police were on the watch for him, attending functions and festivals in safety.

The longer Giuliano survived, the greater his legend grew. Many books and articles were written about him; magazine writers and journalists were escorted to his secret hide-out to interview him face to face; young girls throughout Italy read spurious tales of his passionate love affairs; his photograph was treasured and songs in his praise made him the equivalent of a football hero or a pop singer in the eyes of schoolboys and schoolgirls. Not too much was made of the fact that he and his men were responsible for killing more than a hundred policemen, more than eighty-five civilians—some of these latter for helping the police, some by simple accident. Nor was it emphasised that from ransoms alone this hero of the common man earned an income of £2000 a week.

His continuing success gave Giuliano delusions of grandeur. He was indeed a force to be reckoned with: politicians and landowners were glad to make use of him. So it was easy for him to believe that they wanted him as a popular hero, not simply as the controller of a gang of useful toughs. He came to see himself as Sicily's saviour, and for all his shrewdness was gulled into serving self-regarding politicians who persuaded him they were working solely to bring justice to poverty-stricken, oppressed Sicily. On May Day 1947 he was recruited to attack a communist demonstration in a village outside Palermo—fourteen people were killed including women and children, and more than twenty others were wounded. It lost him a lot of sympathy, but it stood him in good stead with the local bosses, who allowed him to think of himself as another Napoleon or another Mussolini, destined to bring salvation to the island. After all, had fate not baptised him 'Salvatore'—Saviour?

Perhaps it was as well that he did not live to know how he was being exploited. To the end he believed that he had a great mission to accomplish. That is probably the way future legends will remember him, as they did Juro Janosik and Robin Hood, and perhaps it is best so.

The circumstances of Giuliano's end are still argued about and still unresolved. By 1950 the police, though hampered by inefficiency and internal corruption as well as by the non-co-operation of the peasantry, had stepped up their hunt to the extent that every possible move that Giuliano might make was watched. The men he might wish to contact, members of his family, the homes of girls he was known to frequent—all were under constant observation. It was while getting away from a mistress's home in the

The killing of Salvatore Giuliano outside his girlfriend's house.

early morning that he was trapped, shot and killed. Even so, though they claim the credit, the police are not universally allowed it. Many of the accounts claim that it was his twenty-eight year old lieutenant, Pisciotta, who shot him because of some internal feud. There is no doubt that Pisciotta claimed to have killed his chief, nor that Giuliano's mother held Pisciotta responsible. Others add the suggestion of a police deal involving Pisciotta, making him responsible even though it was not his hand that fired the fatal gun. In the corrupt world where private vendettas and competing powers are forever mangling the truth, the facts of Giuliano's death are unlikely ever to be known for certain, nor shall we know who poisoned, or with what motive, Pisciotta in gaol four years later, together with another of Giuliano's former henchmen. The Mafia? Giuliano's family? For revenge? To ensure silence? It is all already part of the mystery that will forever add spice to the legend of Salvatore Giuliano.

Two centuries have passed since Dick Turpin's execution, only a quarter century since Giuliano's killing, yet they both seem to share a world so different from ours that it is almost impossible to imagine either of them surviving today. Is the highwayman species doomed to extinction except in a gradually diminishing number of underdeveloped social environments which still offer sufficient scope for its existence?

I think it highly unlikely. The highwayman has been with us for many hundreds of years in one form or another, and until mankind as a whole experiences a change of heart—which it shows no sign of doing—I think we shall continue to have the highwayman with us—in one form or another. It is only the form which will change. Today's highwaymen are the stocking-masked attackers of the security van, or the meticulous planners who rob the mail train. Both have proved their ability to operate during the past few years, despite the growing sophistication of the ways in which society protects its property. If the police have radio communication, so have the highwaymen; if the police have fast cars and helicopter surveillance, the highwaymen can fight back with new forms of explosive and gas canisters. Technically, crime is keeping pace with crime prevention.

As the number of oppressed peasants in the world diminishes—albeit with agonising slowness—and as we all become property-owners to a greater or lesser extent, the highwayman becomes less of a social hero. He may continue to symbolise individual independence and initiative, but he can hardly be conceived as representing social justice. Films like *Payroll* and *The Great Train Robbery* have considerable appeal, and their protagonists earn the admiration we give to all risk-takers. But we do not see them as anything but thieves, and even a real-life highwayman like Ronald Biggs, the mail-train robber who got away, is hardly a figure of heroic stature, even though we are willing to accord him a certain sympathy as we watch him struggle to evade his pursuers. His story fascinates us; we marvel at the planning of the robbery, the brilliance of its execution, the shrewdness of the subsequent escape. But few of us would want to change places with him or emulate his achievements. Most would agree that he gave up too much for too little.

But there is another class of highwayman who are more promising candidates as heirs to the great tradition—the hijackers. Most crimes run to patterns: there is hardly any form of wrongdoing practised today which wasn't practised a hundred years ago, and very probably long before that. But the hijacking of trains, buses, aircraft and underground trains for ideological motives, is the twentieth century's outstanding contribution to the history of crime. To hold up a plane loaded with passengers, and use them to extort colossal sums of money for a 'good' cause or the release of prisoners, is today's equivalent of robbing the rich to feed the poor, and as such is liable to make the old appeal in new terms. Whether those who do these things are sincere or not is as irrelevant as whether Robin Hood or Juro Janosik or Salvatore Giuliano were sincere. What is important is that they have popular credit for being sincere, and so

Errol Flynn, everybody's idea of the bandit hero.

they become heroes to those who share their political convictions, and to those who believe that political, socially-conscious motives justify any kind of conduct. You may detest them and their methods, as I do, but you must grant them some allowance of respect. Their actions may be atrocious, in logic they can be shown to be as anti-social as they claim them to be social, but we cannot refuse their claim to be ranked somewhat higher in the hierarchy of lawbreakers than the self-regarding burglar or swindler.

Here, of course, lies the danger, a danger which shows itself most vividly in the reports of the attitudes adopted by hijack victims to their kidnappers. When, by capitulation or stratagem, the authorities have ended the stalemate imposed by the hijackers, it is generally found that, for the first few days after their release, their victims are astonishingly sympathetic to their recent captors. They praise their courage, they admire their devotion to their cause;

The highwayman as anti-hero—the hijacker whose prey is the payroll in the security van. (*The Hijacker*)

however alien to their own beliefs. They are grateful for the way they have been treated, however harshly it may have been, and if there was any violence, they find excuses for it. They feel gratitude for any concession, act or even word of kindness, just as poor Cherubini kissed the hand of the bandit who told him he would probably not be murdered.

All this contains more of emotion than of logic, and psychologists have little difficulty in accounting for it. After a few days of normal life, the victims' habitual social values reassert themselves and a natural resentment is likely to replace the unnatural sympathy. But, however transitory and explicable the phenomenon, it is none the less very real and very significant.

The high-minded high-flying highwayman—whose ideological motivations qualify him for a hero's status. (*Victory at Entebbe*)

Our historical survey has enabled us to identify many of the contributory factors which have ensured the enduring popularity of the highwayman. The way in which love and hate, respect and resentment are confused in the hijack victim's mind is characteristic of the ambivalence the public has always felt towards the man whose

172

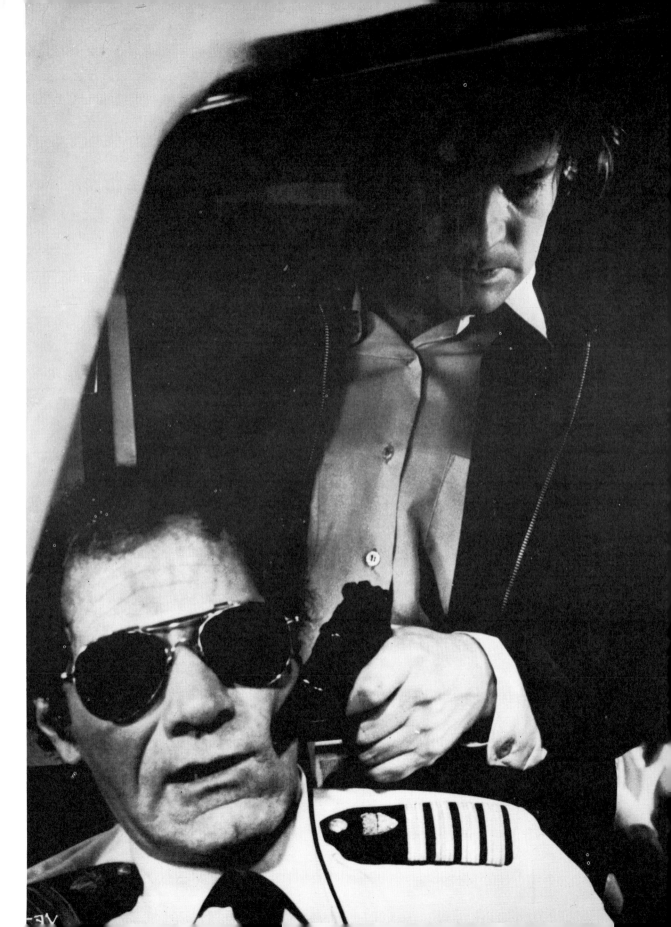

heroism is undoubted, but whose horse is undoubtedly a stolen one. I venture to prophesy that today's hijackers will find a place in the history of highway robbery as enduring as that of any of their predecessors, and that, as she did with Robin Hood and Dick Turpin, with Ned Kelly and Joaquin Murieta, legend will take them into her dressing room, strip them of their sordid everyday gear, give them a good scrubbing, mask out their bruises and blemishes and dress them more becomingly, give them a few lessons in elocution and deportment, then send them out to us again, fit objects now for our admiration and respect, ready to enact the heroic roles we all secretly want them to play.

Index